THE SOCIAL KITCHEN

RECIPES FROM YOUR
FAVOURITE FOOD INFLUENCERS

THE SOCIAL KITCHEN

©2023 Meze Publishing Ltd.
All rights reserved

First edition printed in 2023 in the UK
ISBN: 978-1-915538-08-6

Written by: Kate Reeves-Brown, Katie Fisher & Vicky Frost

Photography by: Timm Cleasby, Paul Gregory & Ellie Grace

Designed by: Phil Turner & Paul Cocker

Sales & PR: Emma Toogood & Lizzy Capps

Printed by Bell and Bain Ltd, Glasgow

Contributors: Kathryn Cornwell, Jenny Jefferies, Corina Blum, Hollie Wood, Karen Wright, Raheel Mirza, Becky Walker, Charlie Jeffreys, Becky Hipkiss, Holly Barnes, Steph Cox, Jen Harrison, Lindsey Willis, Jack Rowbottom, Zak Travess, Natalie Marten, Stuart Snowden & Lucy Parr

Published by Meze Publishing Limited
Unit 1b, 2 Kelham Square
Kelham Riverside
Sheffield S3 8SD
Web: www.mezepublishing.co.uk
Telephone: 0114 275 7709
Email: info@mezepublishing.co.uk

No part of this book shall be reproduced or transmitted in any form or by any means, electronic or mechanical, including photocopying, recording, or by any information retrieval system without written permission of the publisher.

Although every precaution has been taken in the preparation of this work, the publisher and author assume no responsibility for errors or omissions. Neither is any liability assumed for damages resulting from the use of this information contained herein.

STOP SCROLLING & START COOKING

It's no secret that social media has become hugely influential in the world of food and drink, and this book is a celebration of the variety and passion within that movement. Featuring hand-picked contributions from all corners of Instagram's thriving culinary community, The Social Kitchen brings together the people behind all those reels and posts to highlight their skill, talent and love for what they do – putting them in print as a collective for the first time.

We've searched out social media stars sharing their healthy eating journeys; mums and dads experimenting with family-friendly recipes; cooking from the likes of Great British Bake Off contestants and MasterChef: The Professionals finalists; creative ways to manage gut health and gluten-free diets; al fresco inspiration from barbecues to campsites; and much more.

Each contributor has generously shared three of their best recipes for everyone to try at home, and we've also delved into their stories, finding out what makes them tick (or Tok!) and why they love being part of the online foodie phenomenon. Whether you fancy comfort food; something experimental for dinner; a quick and easy air fryer recipe; healthy snacking; or indulgent baking, there's something here for everyone.

We hope you enjoy reading and cooking from The Social Kitchen – whatever your level of experience or confidence in the kitchen, this book aims to inspire you with new and innovative ideas, so stop scrolling and start cooking!

Team Meze x

CONTENTS

@PINCHOFBECKY
IT'S ALL ABOUT BALANCE	10
MAKE-AHEAD BREAKFAST BAGELS	12
DONER-LOADED FLATBREADS	14
CREAMY CHICKEN AND BACON ONE-POT PASTA	16

@INTHELIFEOF_BECKY
FAFF-FREE FOODIE	18
STICKY SESAME CHICKEN NOODLES	20
SRIRACHA HONEY BEEF BOWL	22
CRUNCHY CHEESEBURGER TACOS	24

@CHEFCHARLIEJEFFREYS
FROM DORCHESTER TO… THE DORCHESTER	26
SEARED HALIBUT, SALSIFY AND RAZOR CLAMS	28
PINEAPPLE AND TARRAGON ETON MESS	30
ALL ABOUT LEMON TART	32

@SEARCHINGFORSPICE
SEARCHING FOR SPICE	34
EASY MARINATED GRIDDLED CHICKEN	36
ROASTED CAULIFLOWER CURRY	38
LEMONY AIR FRIED ASPARAGUS WITH ZA'ATAR	40

@BALANCEWITH_HRB
HEALTHY BALANCE	42
SALMON AND RICE BOWLS	44
CREAMY FAJITA BOWLS	46
BLUEBERRY MUFFIN BAKED OATS	48

@DINNER_AT_HOLS
HOLLIE-WOOD DINING	50
SPANISH TRAYBAKE	52
EASY HUNTER'S CHICKEN BURGERS	54
CREAMY PESTO SPAGHETTI AND MEATBALLS	56

@JACKSMEATSHACK
JACK'S MEAT SHACK	58
TOMAHAWK STEAK WITH FIRE ROASTED CHIMICHURRI	60
CHICKEN THIGH FAJITAS WITH PINEAPPLE PICO DE GALLO SALSA	62
TRIPLE-STACKED SMASH BURGERS WITH HOMEMADE SPECIAL SAUCE	64

@AIRFRY_JEN
AIR FRYER QUEEN	66
BREAKFAST MUFFIN	68
CHICKEN AND CHORIZO	70
STEAK AND VEG	72

@JENNYLJEFFERIES
FOR THE LOVE OF THE LAND & SEA	74
LAMB AND SWEET POTATO HOTPOT	76
BANANA LOAF	78
CHOCOLATE PUDDLE PUDDING	80

@KARENWRIGHTBAKE
MEALS ON THE MOVE	84
PROVENCAL CHICKEN	86
MUSHROOM BOURGUIGNON	88
BRATWURST IN BEER WITH STOEMP	90

@NUTRITIONAL_LIFE_LTD_
FOOD FOR HEALTH	92
HEALTHIER FLAPJACK	94
DUCK AND WATERMELON SALAD	96
CREAMY ROASTED TOMATO SOUP	98

@SLIMMING.GYM.AND.GIN
HEALTHY AND HAPPY	100
CHILLI BUTTER CHICKEN	102
SWEET CHILLI PORK	104
HASSELBACK PIZZA STUFFED CHICKEN	106

@LUCYSFRIENDLYFOODS
THE FRIENDLY BAKER	108
SWEETCORN FRITTERS & SPICY TOMATO RELISH	110
LEMON SHERBET DRIZZLE CAKE	112
CRÈME BRÛLÉE WITH SHORTBREAD BITES	114

@WINDSOR__FOODIE
FITNESS, FOOD AND FAMILY	116
LEMONY PRAWN SPAGHETTI	118
SPEEDY BEEF AND PAK CHOI CHOW MEIN	120
SERIOUSLY ADDICTIVE TERIYAKI CHICKEN BITES	122

@RAHEELMIRZACOOKING
COOKALONG CURRIES	124
PRAWN BIRYANI	126
FIVE LENTIL CURRY	128
CHICKEN PALAK	130

@NOTSOFARMERSWIFE
FUSS-FREE FAMILY FOOD	132
ONE-POT ITALIAN SAUSAGE ORZO	134
LAMB PILAF	136
FAKEAWAY KEBAB	138

@GRUMPYNORTHERNFOODIE
WEIRD AND WONDERFUL	142
SPAGHETTI PANCAKES	144
SAUSAGE AND MASH-FILLED YORKSHIRE PUDDING	146
AIR FRYER HUNTER'S CHICKEN POCKETS	148

@ZAKBAKES_
JUNIOR BAKER	150
ROCKY ROAD	152
CHOCOLATE CUPCAKES	154
NO-BAKE VANILLA CHEESECAKE	156

BECKY HIPKISS

IT'S ALL ABOUT BALANCE

Becky Hipkiss started @pinchofbecky back in September 2020 – the pounds had piled on as she turned to food for comfort during lockdown, and she wanted to make some healthy changes to her lifestyle. Her following grew along with her confidence, as she posted daily recipes for healthy home-cooked food and documented her fitness journey.

"I started this journey in September 2020. We were six months into lockdown and I had been diagnosed with mild-moderate depression as a result," explains Becky Hipkiss. "I'm a family person and living over 200 miles away was taking its toll." In lockdown, Becky admits she did what most people did – turned to food. "The only entertainment was the Saturday night takeaway, or the packet of biscuits we ate each day. Literally, we ate a packet of biscuits each day," confesses Becky. "Bourbons."

She started her Instagram account @pinchofbecky as a way to keep herself accountable, as the weightloss and healthy eating community on there is huge. She started with home workouts and eventually braved going to the gym. Becky now leads a healthy, active lifestyle, going to the gym four to five times a week to do a mix of resistance training and cardio. Her main focus now is on getting stronger and being happy and confident in her own skin. Not only does it support her physical health, but her mental health has also reaped the benefits.

Through her Instagram, she loves inspiring and motivating people. Through Instagram, Becky loves inspiring and motivating people by showing the reality of balancing a busy full-time job and socialising while still working towards your goals. She also aims to break down the idea of 'being on a diet' and show that no food is good or bad. You will normally find her either walking round the block in the evening to hit her last steps, batch-cooking on a Sunday or at the 6am gym club most weekdays.

She wants to show people that you don't have to be a fantastic cook or run every day to lose weight or be healthy. Instead, focus on the small changes, which will add up over time. She is known for her fakeaways, protein-packed breakfasts and batch-cooked meals.

"I have built healthy habits that will last a lifetime," says Becky, "and that's my main focus now. To be happy and confident in my own skin. To be able to run without getting too out of breath. To ensure I'm strong for my later years. The gym and the routines I have built also keep my mental health in check." Becky is now training to be a personal trainer, so she can fully understand the impact nutrition and exercise can have on the body.

MAKE-AHEAD BREAKFAST BAGELS

Prep time: 5 minutes | Cook time: 20 minutes | Makes 5 (one for each day of the week)

I'm a bit fussy when it comes to breakfast. I go to the gym first thing in a morning and need something to eat at my desk afterwards. These breakfast bagels have become the most-tagged recipe on my Instagram. They're easy – simply prep them ahead of time and you can customise them however you like. My OG ingredients are the classic sausage and egg, but you can change this up depending on what you fancy. Smoked salmon, cream cheese, a slice of cheese, bacon and hash browns all work well. And it's easy to make them veggie too!

10 low-fat sausages (I prefer Heck chicken sausages for lower calories)
5 eggs
5 bagel thins (or normal bagels)
Sauce of your choice (brown is my fave)

This really is a simple one. Cook your sausages according to the packet instructions. I pop my chicken sausages into my air fryer on 200°c for 15 minutes.

Meanwhile, boil the eggs for 10 minutes until perfectly hard-boiled.

Now for the important bit, set both aside and allow to cool completely – don't peel the eggs.

Once cooled, peel one boiled egg and slice. Slice two sausages in half and toast your bagel.

Now assemble! Top your bagel thin with two sausages, one sliced boiled egg and a squirt of sauce (my fave is HP) – then wrap in foil – the perfect way to transport it out and about. I eat mine cold.

Pop the other sausages and unshelled eggs into an airtight container in the fridge for up to 5 days until ready to assemble the night before work. It just tastes fresher that way!

BECKY HIPKISS

DONER-LOADED FLATBREADS

Prep time: 15 minutes | Cook time: 30 minutes | Serves 2

I love a fakeaway! You should never deprive yourself when healthy eating – it's all about recreating your favourite takeaways as a healthier (usually tastier!) alternative. This is inspired by a late-night kebab after a night out, but is much fresher and a lot lower in calories. Plus it'll take you less time to make this than wait for the takeaway delivery...

250g mince of your choice (I opt for 5% lean beef, but lamb is lovely too)
Salt and black pepper
1 tbsp cumin
1 tsp garlic granules
1 tsp onion powder
1 tsp chilli powder
1 tsp oregano
2 flatbreads

For the pickled salad
50g baby plum tomatoes, diced
1 red onion, diced
½ cucumber, diced
2 tbsp white wine vinegar
1 lemon, juiced
Pinch of sugar

For the tzatziki
½ cucumber, grated
100g Greek yoghurt
½ lemon, juiced
1 clove of garlic, finely chopped

To serve
Chopped parsley
Homemade chips (optional)

Preheat the oven to 200°c.

Pop the mince, a few grinds of salt and pepper and all the dried seasonings into a bowl and mix well (clean hands work well for this or use a food processor if easier). Squeeze into a ball and pop between two sheets of greaseproof paper. Use a rolling pin to roll it out into a thin sheet. Make sure it's nice and thin so it will cook easily. Transfer to a baking tray and pop into the oven for 15 minutes until cooked through (no pink meat).

Meanwhile, let's make the pickled salad. Pop the diced baby tomatoes, red onion and cucumber into a bowl. Add the white wine vinegar, a squeeze of lemon juice and a pinch of sugar. Mix together and set aside.

To make the tzatziki, squeeze any excess water out of the grated cucumber with some kitchen roll. Mix with the Greek yoghurt, a squeeze of lemon juice and the garlic.

About 5 minutes before the meat is ready, pop the flatbreads in the oven to warm through.

Take the kebab meat out of the oven and transfer to a chopping board. Using a pizza cutter or a sharp knife, cut it into strips.

Load the salad onto the flatbreads, top with the slices of meat and drizzle your tzatziki over the top.

To serve, top with fresh parsley and serve with some homemade chips on the side, if you like.

@PINCHOFBECKY

BECKY HIPKISS

CREAMY CHICKEN AND BACON ONE-POT PASTA

Prep time: 10 minutes | Cook time: 30 minutes | Serves 4

This is my favourite batch cook. The key to staying consistent with healthy eating is preparation, in my opinion. I always batch-cook recipes on a Sunday for the week ahead, so I know I have a calorie-counted meal for my lunch that is high in protein and will keep me full. Pasta isn't the enemy when it comes to eating healthily, and this is one of my favourite go-to recipes.

8 bacon rashers, chopped
400g chicken, diced
Cooking oil spray
250g mushrooms, chopped
1 onion, diced
2 cloves of garlic, crushed
150g lighter crème fraîche
70g lighter cream cheese
½ tsp dried parsley
½ tsp dried oregano
½ tsp dried basil
½ tsp chilli flakes
Black pepper
500ml chicken stock
240g dried pasta (I love rigatoni)
100g spinach
50g grated cheese

To serve
Grated parmesan
Chopped parsley

In a big deep pan, add the bacon and chicken and fry with a few sprays of oil for 5 minutes.

Add the mushrooms, onion and garlic. Fry until the meat is cooked through and the onion has softened.

Stir in the crème fraîche, cream cheese, dried herbs, chilli flakes, a few grinds of black pepper and the chicken stock until you get a creamy consistency.

Add the dried pasta and bring to the boil. Simmer for 20 to 25 minutes until the sauce thickens up and the pasta is cooked.

Stir in the spinach until wilted, then sprinkle the grated cheese over and stir in until melted.

To serve, top with a sprinkle of parmesan cheese and fresh parsley if you're feeling fancy.

To save for the week ahead, transfer portions into airtight containers and store in the fridge for up to 4 days. Reheat as needed in the microwave until piping hot. I always add a splash of water before microwaving – it stops it drying out and brings the creaminess back!

BECKY WALKER

FAFF-FREE FOODIE

Becky Walker started her Instagram page @inthelifeof_becky with the main aim of keeping herself accountable for her weight loss goals. Eight years and a baby later, Becky shares her calorie-counted recipes with thousands of followers – fun, colourful, healthy and, most importantly, faff free!

When she created her Instagram account @inthelifeof_becky in 2015, Becky Walker's main goal was to build a space to document her weight loss journey and really hold herself accountable for sticking to her Slimming World plan. When Becky, who is from south Wales, had her daughter in 2019, she turned to social media in the juggle between full-time work, parenting and planning food that would be enjoyed by the whole family.

"When I went back to work after having my daughter Millie, I needed to reframe how I was cooking," explains Becky. "I didn't want to be standing cooking for ages after being at work all day, I needed food that was quick and easy, but that would also enable me to lose weight. That's when I started calorie-counting."

Becky's followers quickly began to multiply and she turned her attention to making all her food look as beautiful and appetising as possible. "I experimented with lots of dishes, things that both my partner and I would enjoy, things my daughter Millie and step-children Lola and Oscar would all eat, things that I hoped would be inspiring to other busy mums who wanted to cook for their family while managing their weight."

Cooking is Becky's space for herself. She loves escaping to the kitchen, away from the pressures of work and family life. Whereas once upon a time cooking was a means to an end, for Becky it is now a source of joy. "I love trying new things, I love creating exciting dishes, but there also has to be no faffing around," Becky jokes. "My food is easy, tasty, colourful and pretty."

You won't find Becky cooking the same meals week in, week out. There is always something new being rustled up in her kitchen, whether it's lunchbox fare for work, quick and easy family dinners, kids' snack boxes or low-calorie sweet treats. She meal plans every week, which is super-popular with her followers, who love the inspiration for faff-free family food and calorie-counted meals.

STICKY SESAME CHICKEN NOODLES

Prep time: 5 minutes | Cook time: 15 minutes | Serves 2-3

This is one of my favourite meals and it's perfect for the whole family. Using store-cupboard staples, this recipe is a one-pan wonder – and it's ready in under 20 minutes!

2 large chicken breasts, diced

1 onion, thinly sliced

1 red pepper, thinly sliced

1 green pepper, thinly sliced

1 tbsp sesame oil

2 tsp paprika

2 tsp garlic granules

4 tbsp soy sauce, plus extra if needed

3 tbsp teriyaki marinade

1 tbsp sesame seeds

600g fresh egg noodles

1 spring onion, finely sliced, to garnish

Add the chicken, onion and peppers to a frying pan with the sesame oil and paprika, then cook for a few minutes until the chicken has browned.

Once browned, add the garlic granules, soy sauce, teriyaki marinade and sesame seeds, and mix together.

Add the fresh egg noodles and mix until the noodles are coated with the marinade (you can add more soy sauce if you need). Once the noodles have cooked, dish up and garnish with the sliced spring onion.

SRIRACHA HONEY BEEF BOWL

Prep time: 2 minutes | Cook time: 15 minutes | Serves 2-3

Sweet with a spicy kick, this meal will be a firm favourite in your house. In a rush? No problem! Whip it up in less than 20 minutes – it's quick, easy and delicious!

150g basmati rice
1 onion, finely chopped
5 spring onions, finely chopped
1 red pepper, finely chopped
1 red chilli, finely chopped
1 tbsp sesame oil
500g lean beef steak mince
1 tsp brown sugar
2 tsp garlic granules
2 tsp ginger
3 tbsp sriracha
4 tbsp soy sauce, plus extra if needed
3 tbsp honey
Salt

To serve
Sriracha
Sriracha mayo
Coriander
Lime wedges

Cook the basmati rice according to the packet instructions.

Meanwhile, add the chopped onion, spring onions, pepper and chilli to a frying pan with the sesame oil and fry for a few minutes until they start to soften. Add the beef mince and fry until browned. Add the brown sugar, garlic, ginger, sriracha, soy sauce and honey.

Once the rice is cooked, drain and add it to the frying pan. Stir to combine and add salt to taste. You can add extra soy sauce if needed.

Dish up and top with sriracha, sriracha mayo and coriander, and serve with lime wedges for squeezing.

BECKY WALKER

CRUNCHY CHEESEBURGER TACOS

Prep time: 5 minutes | Cook time: 30 minutes | Serves 2-3

Fancy a takeaway without the cost? These crunchy cheeseburger tacos will hit the spot! Load them up with your favourite toppings; the only problem you'll have is knowing when to stop…

500g lean beef steak mince
1 red onion, chopped
6 mini white wraps
6 cheese slices
½ lettuce, shredded
10 plum tomatoes, chopped
Jalapeños (optional)
Gherkins (optional)

For the burger sauce
4 tbsp light mayo
4 tbsp ketchup
1 tbsp mild yellow mustard

Mix the burger sauce ingredients together and set aside.

Put the beef mince into a bowl and add half the chopped onion. Once combined, divide the mixture into six equal-sized balls.

Press one ball onto a wrap and press it flat, making sure you spread it out right to the edge of the wrap and it's the same thickness all the way across.

Place a frying pan on a medium-low heat, add the wrap, meat-side down, and cook for 4 minutes, or until the meat is cooked through. Flip it over and add a slice of cheese, then allow this to cook for a few minutes to toast the wrap and melt the cheese.

Repeat for all of the wraps and meat. Once cooked, top with the lettuce, tomatoes, remaining onion and burger sauce, as well as jalapeños and gherkins if you like. Fold in half and feast away!

CHARLIE JEFFREYS

FROM DORCHESTER TO… THE DORCHESTER

Chef Charlie Jeffreys, junior sous chef at the three-Michelin-star restaurant Alain Ducasse at The Dorchester, rose to social media fame when he reached the final of MasterChef: The Professionals in 2022. Now over 11,000 people follow @chefcharliejeffreys on Instagram.

Charlie Jeffreys has cooked for as long as he can remember. Coming from a family of keen cooks, he took inspiration at home from his mum and grandparents, then began working at Yalbury Cottage, a small BnB restaurant near Dorchester in Dorset. He started at the age of 14, initially washing up, but was soon given the chance to get involved with cooking.

"I would really describe my career as a step-by-step process," says Charlie. "From 16 to 18 I worked in Dorset doing my apprenticeship, and then moved to London when I had just turned 18 and started at The Dorchester. I began in The Grill and it was a huge change, moving from a small kitchen with 20 covers to a large busy kitchen with chefs of all nationalities."

After a year, Charlie moved to the acclaimed Alain Ducasse at The Dorchester, the world-famous three-Michelin-star restaurant, and has been there ever since. "It was a whole new experience again," says Charlie, "right down to cutting an onion, everything had to be done in a set way, everything had to be perfect."

After five years working his way up in the three-star kitchen, chef Charlie Jeffreys appeared on BBC's MasterChef: The Professionals in 2022, which is when his social media account really took off.

At home he loves bread-making and has done some videos on his Instagram page @chefcharliejeffreys featuring his favourite sourdough recipes, which he dedicated a lot of time to during lockdown. True to his Dorset roots, he's also fond of cooking with fish and says it is his favourite section at work. "I love fishing, I love the sea, I love fish," says Charlie. "I love catching it, I love cooking it, I love eating it."

You'll find plenty of delicious fish recipes on his Instagram page, and he has supplied a fabulous halibut recipe here, which showcases his philosophy of how you can make the most stunning dishes when you source beautiful ingredients.

CHARLIE JEFFREYS

SEARED HALIBUT, SALSIFY AND RAZOR CLAMS

Prep time: 2 hours | Cook time: 2 hours | Serves 5

The best ingredients make the best recipes! This is not the easiest ingredients list to get your hands on, but if you can venture down to your local fishmongers and grocery market to search out these wonderful ingredients you will not regret it.

200g samphire, + 50g to serve
70ml olive oil
5 halibut fillets, skins removed
80g salted butter
Salt and black pepper

For the salsify
13 whole pieces of salsify, peeled (keep the tops and peel)
570ml vegetable stock
200ml cream
260g unsalted butter
1 clove of garlic
2 sprigs of thyme

For the razor clams
½ shallot, thinly sliced
½ bulb of fennel, thinly sliced
1 clove of garlic
8 razor clams, cleaned
50ml white wine

For the sauce
½ bulb of fennel, chopped
½ shallot, roughly chopped
50g unsalted butter
2g black peppercorns
1 clove of garlic
100g mussels
100ml white wine
1 litre vegetable stock

Pick the bottoms off the samphire (save these) so you're left with the tender green top. Chop roughly and blitz until smooth, adding 50ml olive oil slowly to make a pesto. Set aside. For the salsify purée, roughly chop eight salsify and sweat in a pan with 1 teaspoon olive oil on a high heat until it starts to colour, then deglaze with the stock and bring to the boil. Add the cream and cook on a medium heat until very soft. Blend with 60g butter until smooth. Set aside and keep warm. Preheat the oven to 180°C. Cut the remaining five salsify into 5cm sticks. Heat 1 teaspoon olive oil in a pan on a high-medium heat, add the salsify and keep them moving in the pan. Add the remaining 200g butter, the garlic and thyme, and cook until coloured. Put the pan into the oven and cook for 8 to 10 minutes until soft. Drain from the butter and set aside. Use the reserved salsify peelings to make salsify chips. Preheat the oven to 160°C. Rub the skins with oil, salt and pepper and arrange on a lined tray. Cook for 1 hour until crispy.

For the razor clams, sweat the shallot, fennel and garlic with 1 teaspoon olive oil over a medium heat until softened, then fill the pan with water, bring everything to the boil and add the clams. When they have opened fully, remove with a slotted spoon and let cool. Discard the water. Once cool, remove the white from the shell, cutting away the brown parts. Slice thinly and store in the fridge. For the sauce, heat 1 teaspoon olive oil in a pan with the reserved ends of salsify and samphire and add the fennel and shallot. Sweat it to give them a little colour, then add the butter and continue to colour all the vegetables. Add the peppercorns and garlic, then add the mussels. Turn up the temperature to high and deglaze the pan with the white wine. Cover and cook until the mussels have opened up, then add the stock and cook for 20 minutes. Pass the stock through a fine-mesh sieve, then add a couple of spoons of salsify purée to make a sauce.

Season the halibut with salt and preheat the oven to 180°C. Heat 1 teaspoon olive oil in a pan, add the halibut and cook until golden (2 minutes on each side). Add the butter and, once foaming, baste and finish in the oven for 5 minutes. Drain and rest for a couple of minutes. Serve as pictured.

@CHEFCHARLIEJEFFREYS

CHARLIE JEFFREYS

PINEAPPLE AND TARRAGON ETON MESS

Prep time: 1 hour | Cook time: 2 hours | Serves 8

This has to be my favourite combination out of all of my recipes, so trust me on this one! This is a twist on a classic summer dessert, looks great and is proper refreshing. If you don't have an ice cream machine, you can always use a shop-bought sorbet.

For the pineapple balls
½ pineapple, skin removed
100ml pineapple juice
10g ginger, peeled and sliced

For the meringue
100g each egg whites, caster sugar, icing sugar & melted white chocolate

For the pineapple salad
½ pineapple, skin removed
2 sprigs of tarragon, chopped
2 limes, segmented

For the sorbet
150ml milk & 115ml water
13g milk powder
30g dextrose & 4g stabiliser
85g glucose powder/syrup
90g sugar & 10g tarragon
130ml each lime & lemon juice

For the cream
200ml cream
2 tsp icing sugar
1 tsp vanilla paste, or seeds from ½ pod

For the decoration
3 sprigs of tarragon

For the pineapple balls, use a melon baller to scoop 16 spheres out of the pineapple, 2 for each portion. Heat up the pineapple juice with the slices of peeled ginger. Pour this over the pineapple balls and cover with cling film.

For the meringue, line a baking tray with parchment and preheat the oven to 90°c. Whisk the egg whites to stiff peaks. Slowly add three quarters of the caster sugar while whisking. When incorporated, add the rest and then fold in the icing sugar by hand. Transfer the meringue to a piping bag and pipe eight 5cm circles on the lined baking tray. Cook in the oven for 1 hour until the outer shell is hard. Pick each meringue up very carefully and scoop out the bottom – you should be left with a hollow meringue ready to be filled. Put back in the oven for a further hour to crisp up.

Once cooked, brush with melted white chocolate to make sure the meringue won't soak up the filling. Leave in a cool space (not in the fridge).

For the pineapple salad, dice the pineapple into small cubes and place in a bowl. Add the chopped tarragon and lime segments.

For the sorbet, put all the ingredients except the tarragon, lime and lemon juices into a pan and bring to the boil, then let the mixture cool down. Once cool, blend with the tarragon leaves. Add the lime juice and lemon juice. Put into an ice cream machine to churn.

For the cream, whisk the cream to soft peaks with the sugar and vanilla.

For the decoration, line a plate with cling film tightly and rub a very small amount of oil on the cling film. Pick individual tarragon leaves from the sprigs and place on the plate, then cover tightly with more cling film. Microwave for 1 minute on high. You should be left with crispy leaves.

To serve, turn your meringues over so the hole is facing up, then add a small scoop of sorbet in the hole. Top this with the salad, then the cooked balls of pineapple. Cover everything with some cream and then turn it over quickly onto a plate so you are left with just the meringue and all the goodness hidden underneath. Top the meringue with more cream and the crispy tarragon.

@CHEFCHARLIEJEFFREYS

CHARLIE JEFFREYS

ALL ABOUT LEMON TART

Prep time: 1 hour | Cook time: 2 hours | Makes 6

This is no ordinary lemon tart. It is super sour, super lemony and super delicious. With a simple and easy-to-mould pastry and lots of different lemon elements, it is a perfect dessert for a wake-me-up with a cup of tea, or an afternoon snack, or even a late-night indulgence.

For the pastry
120g unsalted butter, softened
80g sugar & 40g eggs
200g plain flour
2g salt
30g ground almonds

For the almond sponge
100g unsalted butter, softened
100g icing sugar
135g ground almonds
100g eggs

For the lemon curd
50g lemon juice
15g lime juice
1 lemon, zested
105g eggs & 75g sugar
55g unsalted butter

For the meringue
100g egg whites
100g caster sugar
100g icing sugar
1 lemon & 1 lime, zested

For the decoration
2 lemons & 100g sugar
100ml water
Lemon balm leaves
1½ limes, zested

For the pastry, put the butter and sugar in a stand mixer fitted with the paddle attachment. Add the eggs and mix. Finally, without beating too much, add the flour, salt and almonds. Bring it together and turn out onto a flour-dusted surface. Roll the pastry into a flat circle, cover with cling film and put in the fridge to chill for 30 minutes.

Grease six 8cm tart tins and preheat the oven to 160°c. Divide the pastry into six balls (75g each) and roll each out to 3mm thick. Use the pastry circles to line the tart tins and cut away the excess around the top. Cook in the preheated oven for 10 to 15 minutes until a very light golden brown. Leave to cool. For the almond sponge, mix all the ingredients together in a stand mixer or by hand. Spoon or pipe roughly 20g into the base of each cooled tart case, leaving space for it to rise. Cook for 6 to 8 minutes until the pastry and sponge are golden brown.

For the lemon curd, heat the lemon and lime juice with the lemon zest on a medium heat. Whip the eggs and sugar together, then add the warm juice slowly while whisking. Put this mix back on the stove and mix over a low heat for 8 minutes. Transfer to a blender, add the butter and blend for 5 minutes. It should coat the back of a spoon. Spoon or pipe this onto the top of your tarts and then leave in the fridge for 30 minutes.

For the meringue, whip the egg whites in a stand mixer and slowly add half the sugar. Once stiff, add the rest of the sugar and keep mixing. Once stable, remove from the mixer and gently fold in the icing sugar. Line a baking tray with acetate or parchment and pipe or spoon small dots onto the lined tray, then, with the tip of a damp spoon, push down and away from the dot. Grate the lemon and lime zest over the tops. Preheat the oven to 90°c and cook the meringues for 30 minutes and then leave on the side somewhere warm. For the decoration, segment the lemons, removing the pith and seeds. Put the water and sugar in a pan and bring to the boil. Pour over the lemon segments. Take the tarts from the fridge and decorate each one with nine or ten meringues, five lemon segments strained from the liquid and finally some lemon balm leaves and the grated zest of ¼ lime.

CORINA BLUM

SEARCHING FOR SPICE

Starting life as a hobby 12 years ago, @searchingforspice has grown from a diary-style blog to a highly successful Instagram account followed by over 13,000 food lovers. Its creator Corina Blum shares her passion for flavour, taking inspiration from all over the world.

Before she became a mum, Corina Blum taught English as a foreign language and spent her spare time cooking, reading about and thinking about food. Once her youngest started school, she found the time to add writing about and photographing food to this list. She started a blog, Searching for Spice, which became somewhere she could put her recipes down in one place, accompanied by – what she now jokingly refers to as – terribly shot photos.

Food photography became as much of a passion for her as the recipes. Fast-forward a decade and Corina's blog – and now Instagram page @searchingforspice – is a vibrant showcase of stunning food photography and videos, which has seen her partner with big-name brands to bring recipes to life.

Corina brought her blog to Instagram in 2016 and began to create a delightfully appetising grid of family-friendly recipes, busting with colour and flavour. "I chose the name @searchingforspice even though I didn't really like spicy food when I was younger," Corina confesses. "My husband introduced me to spice, and my own love for spices then developed at the same time as my love for cooking, so it feels to me like the two go hand-in-hand."

Corina takes inspiration from around the world for her dishes, bringing together her love of spices and her desire to create food that her whole family will enjoy. Her children both enjoy trying dishes with plenty of spice, so Corina focuses on meals that fit in with busy family lifestyles.

"I love creating useful recipes for other busy parents," explains Corina, "so I think about food that works with people eating at different times, food that will appeal to picky kids as well as adults, and food that can be put together quickly after work and school. I love air fryer recipes as they are really useful for getting things cooked quickly."

Corina has worked with a plethora of brands that fit with her approach to cooking, such as Knorr, Very Lazy, Deli Kitchen, Lingham's and Roi Thai. She chooses brands that help people to deliver flavour in their cooking and get healthy food onto plates quickly and easily. With thousands of followers looking for easy-to-make and adaptable recipes, there are sure to be lots more partnerships in the future.

CORINA BLUM

EASY MARINATED GRIDDLED CHICKEN

Prep time: 5 minutes, plus at least 1 hour marinating | Cook time: 12 minutes | Serves 4

I always feel an easy way to make a simple piece of meat really tasty is to make a great marinade for it. If I haven't planned dinner, but have some chicken in the fridge, this dish is often the recipe I resort to. I love to serve this on a flatbread with salad, or with chips.

4 chicken breasts
4 cloves of garlic, crushed
1 tsp ground cumin
1 tsp cayenne pepper
1 tsp ground coriander
½ tsp smoked paprika
¼ tsp salt
1 lemon, juiced
1 tbsp olive oil, plus extra for brushing

Butterfly the chicken breasts by cutting them in half horizontally and opening them out.

Mix together all the other ingredients in a bowl for the marinade. Put the chicken in the container with the marinade and make sure it is coated on all sides. Cover and place in the fridge for at least an hour, but up to 24 hours.

Take the chicken out of the fridge 20 minutes before cooking to allow it to come to room temperature.

Brush a griddle pan with a little oil. When it is hot, place the butterflied marinated chicken on the pan. Cook for 6 minutes, then turn over and continue to cook until cooked through (double-check the chicken is cooked through by cutting into the thickest part of one of the pieces).

Remove from the pan and allow to rest for a few moments, before serving with your choice of sides.

CORINA BLUM

ROASTED CAULIFLOWER CURRY

Prep time: 20 minutes | Cook time: 30 minutes | Serves 4

I love this curry as it is so versatile. The cauliflower is lightly spiced and roasted, and then served with the sauce. You can adapt it by serving the sauce with other roasted vegetables or even with meat. It's also a great recipe for serving with leftover roast chicken.

1 cauliflower, cut into 5cm pieces
1 tbsp vegetable oil, plus extra for greasing
½ tsp paprika
½ tsp cayenne pepper
½ tsp ground turmeric
¼ tsp ground cinnamon
2 tbsp coriander leaves, to serve
Rice and pickles, to serve

For the sauce
1 onion, roughly chopped
1 tbsp roughly chopped root ginger
5 cloves of garlic
1-2 chilli peppers, to taste
2 tbsp vegetable oil
1 x 400g tin of chopped tomatoes
2 tsp ground coriander
2 tsp garam masala
1 tsp ground cumin
1 tsp cayenne pepper
½ tsp ground turmeric

Preheat the oven to 180°C. Lightly oil a baking tray.

Put the cauliflower pieces, oil and all the spices in a bowl and mix well to coat. Arrange on the lightly oiled baking tray. Roast in the preheated oven for 25 minutes, turning over halfway through. You can also air fry the cauliflower; it'll take about 15 to 20 minutes at 180°C.

For the sauce, blitz the onion, ginger, garlic and chilli pepper(s) in a food processor, and then transfer to a saucepan with the oil. Fry gently for about 5 minutes. While they are cooking, blitz the tinned tomatoes in the blender.

Stir the dried spices into the onion mixture, plus a tablespoon of water if the paste seems too dry, and cook, stirring, for a couple of minutes.

Stir in the blitzed tomatoes. Bring up to the boil, then lower to a simmer and cook for 20 minutes.

Serve the roasted cauliflower with the curry sauce, topped with some coriander leaves. I also like to have some pickles and rice on the side.

@SEARCHINGFORSPICE

CORINA BLUM

LEMONY AIR FRIED ASPARAGUS WITH ZA'ATAR

Prep time: 2-3 minutes | Cook time: 5 minutes | Serves 4

I love how quickly asparagus cooks in the air fryer – it gets these delightful crispy bits around the edges. Serving it with za'atar and lemon juice really brings out its flavour. It's a lovely side dish with fish or meat, or it can even be a vegetarian starter.

200g asparagus
2 tsp olive oil
½ lemon, juiced
1 tsp za'atar
Pinch of salt (optional; some za'atar brands contain salt)

Break any woody ends off the asparagus, then toss with the oil to coat. Put the asparagus in a preheated air fryer at 180°c and air fry for 5 minutes.

When the asparagus is ready, take it out of the air fryer, squeeze over the lemon juice and sprinkle over the za'atar and salt, if using. Serve at once.

HOLLY BARNES

HEALTHY BALANCE

30-year-old Holly Barnes is all about finding balance in life. She started her Instagram page @balancewith_hrb when she decided to become fitter and healthier, and finally find an achievable lifestyle after years of fad diets and a binge-restrict mindset – now she inspires others to do the same.

Holly started her page @balancewith_hrb in 2021 after struggling with an unhealthy approach towards food. She has always loved cooking. Having been diagnosed with coeliac disease at the age of four, Holly was used to cooking from scratch. However she had fallen into a cycle of yo-yo dieting, which she was determined to break for good.

"When I first started my Instagram page, I did it as sort of a food diary," explains Holly, "and this gave me some accountability for my weight loss." In fact, Holly's page began life under the name @slimmingwith_hrb and was all about her weight loss goals. As her followers multiplied and Holly's journey continued, her page grew organically, and it gradually transitioned into a collection of food, fitness and self-love.

Under its new name @balancewith_hrb Holly's page has acquired over 40,000 followers, ranging from coeliacs and those with gluten intolerances to those looking for fitness inspiration and health positivity. "It's all about good food with no restrictions," says Holly, who shares lunch prep inspiration, low-calorie dinners, high-protein meals and plenty of judgement-free healthy mindset advice.

For Holly, balance is about being able to eat healthily and also being able to go out and enjoy social occasions; it's about looking after your body and mind, it's about following a gluten-free diet and not missing out on anything.

"As well as coeliac disease, I was recently told I have IBS, so have had to cut out more foods from my diet," says Holly. "I want to show on my page @balancewith_hrb that coeliac disease, IBS or food allergies do not have to restrict you. And most importantly, that healthy, nutritious food should never be boring!"

SALMON AND RICE BOWLS

Prep time: 15 minutes | Cook time: 15-20 minutes | Serves 2

Full of flavour, filling and delicious, this is an accidental throw-together meal that turned out to be one of our favorites!

2 skinless salmon fillets (approx. 230g)
140g plain white rice
200g tender stem broccoli
100g cucumber, chopped
20g sweet chilli mayo
2 tsp water

For the sauce
20g runny honey
20g sweet chilli sauce
10ml gluten-free soy sauce
1 tsp ground ginger
15g cornflour

Preheat the oven or an air fryer to 190°c.

Cut the salmon into bite-size pieces and place on some greaseproof paper on an oven tray, and cook in the oven or air fryer for 15 minutes.

Meanwhile, cook the rice according to the packet instructions and cook the broccoli in boiling water for 10 minutes.

Place a saucepan over a low heat and add the sauce ingredients. Mix well until combined, thick and sticky.

Place the rice into a bowl and carefully add the salmon pieces on top, along with the broccoli and cucumber. Pour the sauce over the salmon pieces.

Mix together the sweet chilli mayo and water, then drizzle it over the whole dish. Enjoy!

CREAMY FAJITA BOWLS

Prep time: 10 minutes | Cook time: 15 minutes | Serves 2

Probably the simplest and quickest dish I make, this recipe is perfect for when you are short on time and need a quick dinner. I used lettuce, tomatoes and cucumber here, but feel free to use whatever salad ingredients you like.

300g baby potatoes, halved
300g chicken breast, cut into chunks
1 red pepper, chopped
Cooking oil spray
150g crème fraîche
1 tbsp fajita seasoning
160g iceberg lettuce, shredded
100g cucumber, chopped
6 cherry tomatoes, halved
2 spring onions, chopped

Preheat the oven or air fryer to 190°c.

Cook the halved potatoes in boiling water for 10 minutes before draining and adding to an oven tray or air fryer. Oven bake or air fry for 15 minutes.

Meanwhile, add the add the chicken and pepper to a heated frying pan with a couple of sprays of oil and cook over a medium heat, stirring often.

Once the chicken is cooked, add the crème fraîche and fajita seasoning and mix well so all of the chicken and peppers are coated.

Divide the salad between two bowls and add the crispy new potatoes. Add the chicken mix on top of the salad and enjoy!

HOLLY BARNES

BLUEBERRY MUFFIN BAKED OATS

Prep time: 10 minutes | Cook time: 15 minutes | Serves 2

The perfect sweet treat for breakfast, this dish is easy to prep in advance and tastes delicious, plus it's gluten- and dairy-free. It took many failed attempts to perfect this recipe!

60g gluten-free oats
35g vanilla protein powder
1 tsp cinnamon
1 tsp baking powder
1 medium egg
100g vegan plain yoghurt
Splash of water
40g blueberries

Preheat the oven or air fryer to 180°c.

In a mixing bowl add the oats, protein powder, cinnamon, baking powder, egg and yoghurt, and mix well. The mixture will be thick, so add a splash of water (about 4 teaspoons) to loosen it and mix again. Add the blueberries and fold them into the mixture.

Divide the mixture between two small ovenproof dishes and air fry or oven bake for 15 minutes.

Once cooked you can enjoy straight away or let cool and take to work the following day.

HOLLIE WOOD

HOLLIE-WOOD DINING

Social media sensation, culinary expert, and mum of two, Hollie Wood enjoys creating healthy recipes that suit a family lifestyle. She has inspired many on their own cooking journeys through her wildly successful Instagram account where she shares her secrets for cooking quick and easy family meals.

Hollie inherited her love of cooking from her mum, who was a constant presence in the kitchen while she was growing up. From the age of 11, she was given the task (or, for her, the joy) of cooking Thursday night dinner, which inspired her love of trying new flavour combinations and recipes.

This love of food continued strongly into Hollie's own family; her husband Steve and her children Harry and Lottie are all big foodies too, and they love to cook together and try new things in the kitchen. Now, as a skilled culinary expert with over 15 years of experience, Hollie runs a successful Instagram account to inspire others to make easy and delicious family-friendly meals. Aware of the struggle many of us have when thinking of new ideas for meals the whole family will enjoy, Hollie aims to lighten the load and provide inspiration.

Her Instagram account, @dinner_at_hols, began during lockdown as a way for Hollie to journal her homemade meals and her journey. People loved her creative, quick, and nutritious recipes that suited a busy-parent lifestyle, so much so that her growing following allowed Hollie to pursue her foodie career full-time. With a combined following of over 200k across Instagram and TikTok, it's clear that people adore her delicious recipes and meal ideas. "I couldn't quite believe it when I started receiving messages from people who have tried and loved my recipes – it is the best feeling in the world!" Hollie explains.

Dinner at Hol's is not just the name of her Instagram account; she is currently publishing a book of the same name, which is due to be released in the autumn of 2023. The recipes she has included in The Social Kitchen are just a teaser of what can be discovered in her upcoming cookbook, which contains over 80 family-sized, calorie-counted recipes. It offers everything from one pot wonders and personal family favourites to snacks and sides, all of them designed by Hollie with nutrition and affordability in mind. She even suggests alterations and additions to cater for fussy little ones! If you like this brief glimpse into Hollie's world of speedy, family-friendly cooking, keep an eye out for the upcoming Dinner at Hol's and make sure you check out her online presence in the meantime.

HOLLIE WOOD

SPANISH TRAYBAKE

Prep time: 5 minutes | Cook time: 40 minutes | Serves 4

This recipe is a dinner I've been making for years. I love the smoky flavours in this dish, and it is just so simple to make. It's perfect for a summer's evening, enjoyed in the garden with a glass of sangria.

500g baby potatoes
3 peppers, sliced
1 red onion, sliced
600g chicken thighs
50g chorizo, sliced
3 cloves of garlic, finely grated
2 tbsp smoked paprika
1 tbsp ground coriander
1 tbsp garlic granules
½ tsp chilli flakes
½ tsp sugar or sweetener
½ tsp salt
4 tbsp light mayonnaise
Fresh parsley, to garnish

Preheat the oven to 200°c. Cut the baby potatoes evenly into quarters so that they're all similar in size.

Put the potatoes in a large ovenproof dish along with the peppers, onion, chicken thighs, chorizo, 2 cloves of garlic, all the seasonings, sugar, and salt.

Mix well and then place the dish into the oven for 40 minutes until the potatoes and chicken are cooked through.

While that's cooking, make the aioli by mixing the remaining clove of garlic into the mayonnaise along with a pinch of salt and a tiny bit of water, until it's a loose consistency.

Once the traybake is cooked, remove from the oven, and drizzle the aioli on top.

Garnish with some fresh parsley, then serve and enjoy.

Tip:

This dinner is so delicious when served with crusty bread for mopping up all those juices. I buy the mini bake-at-home baguettes that are usually about 140 calories each.

HOLLIE WOOD

EASY HUNTER'S CHICKEN BURGERS

Prep time: 5 minutes | Cook time: 25 minutes | Serves 4

Sticky, smoky BBQ sauce, crispy bacon, juicy chicken, and melty gooey cheese! What more can you want from a burger? These easy burgers are perfect for a midweek treat or a tasty 'fakeaway' when you want something that takes little effort but has maximum flavour.

4 chicken thighs
1 tbsp smoked paprika
½ tbsp garlic granules
½ tbsp oregano
1 tsp salt
4 rashers of bacon
4 tbsp BBQ sauce
60g cheddar cheese, grated
4 brioche burger buns

Preheat the oven to 220°C/200°C fan or 190°C if using an air fryer.

On a flat surface, bash your chicken thighs with a rolling pin until they are thinner and even in size.

Season the chicken with the smoked paprika, garlic granules, oregano and salt.

Lay the bacon on top of the flattened chicken thighs, then put them in the oven or air fryer for 15 minutes.

Spread the BBQ sauce and cheese on top of the bacon wrapped chicken, then cook for another 10 minutes or until the chicken is cooked through.

Meanwhile, toast the brioche burger buns cut sides down in a dry frying pan to crisp them up.

Assemble the burgers with a cheesy chicken thigh inside each brioche bun. Serve and enjoy.

Tip:

You can always swap the thighs for chicken breast if you prefer. Just make sure to reduce the cooking time slightly so the breasts don't dry out and stay moist.

HOLLIE WOOD

CREAMY PESTO SPAGHETTI AND MEATBALLS

Prep time: 5 minutes | Cook time: 15 minutes | Serves 4

My kids absolutely love spaghetti and meatballs, so this always goes down well with them. It's a quick and easy dinner too and can be achieved in just 20 minutes: perfect after a busy day.

20 small meatballs (approximately)
300g spaghetti
Salt and pepper, to taste
1 red onion, finely diced
2 cloves of garlic, grated
1 tbsp tomato purée
4 tbsp red or green pesto
200ml hot chicken stock
120ml light single cream
60g cheddar, finely grated
Fresh basil, to garnish

Start by frying the meatballs in a large pan for around 10 minutes.

Meanwhile, put the spaghetti into a pan of boiling water with a generous amount of salt.

Add the onion to the pan with the meatballs and cook until soft.

Stir in the garlic and cook for another minute.

Add the tomato purée and pesto to the pan and cook for another minute or so.

Pour in the stock and cream, then allow the sauce to reduce.

Once the meatballs are cooked through, check the seasoning and adjust as needed, then add the spaghetti to the meatballs and sauce along with a little pasta water.

Give this a good mix, adding more pasta water until you get the perfect silky consistency.

Garnish with the grated cheese and fresh basil. Serve and enjoy.

Tip:

For an alternative to shop-bought meatballs, you can always use sausage meat rolled into little balls, or even make your own meatballs from scratch.

JACK ROWBOTTOM

JACK'S MEAT SHACK

Barbecue enthusiast, content creator and producer of a range of spice rubs, Jack Rowbottom left his career with the police to become one of Instagram's favourite barbecue chefs – @jacksmeatshack – known for his passion for cooking over fire.

Jack Rowbottom had worked for the Metropolitan Police for 15 years before he made the move to being a full-time grill master. He'd always been a keen cook and remembers his nan's cooking with fondness – from sausage and homemade chips to her famous pastry-encased meat patties. "I remember the first meal I cooked for my parents was chicken thighs stuffed with sausage meat and pistachios, wrapped in bacon," says Jack. "It was from Gordon Ramsay's World Kitchen: Recipes From The F Word. I remember saving up and going to buy the ingredients so I could cook it for them."

He actually never had a barbecue as a child and was introduced to the cooking technique by a friend's Italian family. Once he discovered this way of cooking, his eyes were opened. "My friends and I started to barbecue, and we'd do it whatever the weather – in the cold, in the wet," he remembers. "We'd spend a lot on ingredients and really put everything into it."

He started the Instagram account under the name @jacksmeatshack with a Father's Day post in June 2014. "It was a terrible picture looking back," laughs Jack, but his page has come a long way since then. For Jack's birthday that year, his wife Hayley registered the name Jack's Meat Shack and got a logo designed – the same logo he still uses to this day.

He began contacting brands and was soon working with big names such as Traeger Grills and Lidl. On both Instagram and TikTok, his following flourished and @jacksmeatshack has grown to a point where he left his job with the police in July 2022. Since then his wife Hayley has left her job to come on board, juggling the business with taking care of their daughters Ivy, aged three (named after Jack's food inspiration, his nan), and Remi, aged one.

In a bid to create the best dishes possible, Jack has created a range of multi-purpose spice mixes. Herby, earthy or fiery, Jack has created a seasoning mix for the job, and you'll see them put to delicious use in the recipes overleaf.

Not content with just running his own successful social media account, Jack created the company Mighty Bear Media (@mighty_bear_media) to offer content creation and social media management for a variety of businesses, with the aim to offer a leg up to like-minded entrepreneurs and creators looking for a change in career and to follow their passions.

Portrait: @micksabeyvisuals

TOMAHAWK STEAK WITH FIRE ROASTED CHIMICHURRI

Prep time: 20 minutes | Cook time: 1 hour 30 minutes | Serves 2-4 (depending on size of the steak)

Steak on the bone is just next-level delicious. Packed with inter-muscular fat, which means plenty of flavour, it's definitely a barbecue showstopper. Here it is served with my fire-roasted chimichurri, which takes any steak to new heights – my absolute favourite steak side dish.

1 tomahawk steak
Jack's Meat Shack Cowboy Coffee (multi-purpose seasoning)

For the chimichurri
1 red pepper
4 tomatoes
5 spring onions
1 red onion
1 red chilli
50g parsley
4 tbsp olive oil
2 tbsp red wine vinegar
Salt and black pepper

To make the chimichurri, prepare the barbecue for cooking on direct heat. Place the red pepper, tomatoes, spring onions, red onion and red chilli in a roasting tray. Cook on the barbecue over direct heat until the skin on the pepper turns black and the other vegetables are charred.

Remove from the grill and cover the whole tray with foil to allow the vegetables to sweat. Once cooled enough to handle, remove the burnt skins from the pepper and onion and discard the outer layers, seeds and stalks from everything else. Don't worry too much if a little char remains on the flesh; it will only add flavour. Add all the ingredients to a food processor and add the parsley, olive oil, red wine vinegar, and salt and pepper. Blitz until smooth. Set aside while you cook the steak.

To cook your tomahawk steak, set up the barbecue for indirect cooking and stabilise the temperature at 135°c.

Remove the steak from its packaging and pat it dry with a paper towel. Lightly score the outer surface of the steak with a sharp knife in a diamond pattern. This will enable your seasoning to penetrate the flesh of the meat deeper. Season with plenty of Cowboy Coffee – don't be shy and ensure it is covered all over to create a tasty bark.

Add a lump of smoking wood directly into the coals to give that extra level of smoky flavour. Smoke the steak on the barbecue until it reaches your desired internal cooking temperature.

Remove the steak from the barbecue and leave it to rest for around 20 minutes. Rake the charcoal to remove any settled ash and get the charcoal nice and hot before laying the steak directly onto it. Cook for 1 minute on each side, then remove from the barbecue. Slice and enjoy with the chimichurri.

JACK ROWBOTTOM

CHICKEN THIGH FAJITAS WITH PINEAPPLE PICO DE GALLO SALSA

Prep time: 20 minutes | Cook time: 20 minutes | Serves 4

Fajitas are particularly special for me, as it was the first meal I cooked for my (now) wife. Now it is a weekly staple in our household and we eat it as a family. We love that it is a meal that we can all dig into and build at the dinner table.

8 boneless chicken thighs
Jack's Meat Dust (multi-purpose seasoning)
1 tbsp oil
1 red pepper, thinly sliced
1 large white onion, thinly sliced
2 cloves of garlic, minced
8 small flour tortilla wraps

For the salsa
1 pineapple, cut into wedges
2 large tomatoes, finely chopped
1 red onion, finely chopped
Handful of coriander, finely chopped
1 red chilli, deseeded and finely chopped
2 limes, zested and juiced
¼ tsp salt

Preheat the barbecue to 200°c and set it up for direct grilling.

Coat the chicken thighs all over in Jack's Meat Dust. Place the chicken thighs over the heat and grill until coloured, then flip and cook on the other side. Remove from the grill once the thighs reach 75°c.

Allow to rest for a few minutes before slicing into strips.

To make the pico de gallo salsa, grill the pineapple on the barbecue until lightly charred, approximately 10 minutes. Remove from the heat and finely dice. Allow the pineapple to cool, then add to a mixing bowl with the tomatoes, red onion, coriander, chilli, lime zest and juice, and salt, then mix.

To make the fajita vegetables, preheat a cast-iron pan over the barbecue with the oil. Add the pepper, onion and minced garlic, and cook, stirring occasionally so they don't stick, until al dente but cooked through.

To assemble the fajitas, add strips of chicken to a flour tortilla and add a good helping of fajita vegetables. Add an even better helping of pineapple pico de gallo salsa. Tuck in and enjoy with friends and family.

JACK ROWBOTTOM

TRIPLE-STACKED SMASH BURGERS WITH HOMEMADE SPECIAL SAUCE

Prep time: 20 minutes | Cook time: 10 minutes | Serves 4

Burgers have always held a special place in my heart. However, when I was first introduced to the In-N-Out Burger from the Californian fast food chain I was smitten! This is my take on a homemade version on the barbecue.

1 red onion, thinly sliced
2 tomatoes, sliced
Sea salt
1.2kg good-quality beef mince (20/80 fat ratio works best)
12 cheese slices
1 tbsp finely chopped jalapeños
4 burger buns
1 iceberg lettuce, shredded

For the special sauce
100g mayonnaise
2 tbsp tomato ketchup
1 gherkin, finely chopped
¼ white onion, finely chopped

Mix all the ingredients for the special sauce together and set aside.

Soak the sliced red onion in cold water. This will make it crunchy and remove the harsh raw onion taste. Sprinkle the tomato slices with salt and set aside.

Preheat the barbecue to 230°c, ensuring there is a flat surface inserted (such as a cast-iron plate). Roll the mince into 12 balls of 100g each.

When the grill has reached the correct cooking temperature, place each ball onto the flat surface and, as the name suggests, smash the patties flat with a burger press. Aim for an even 1cm thickness. Allow to cook for around 60 seconds before flipping.

Once flipped, season the patty with sea salt, top with a slice of burger cheese and sprinkle with chopped jalapeño.

Allow to cook for another 60 seconds, or until they have reached an internal cooking temperature of 55°c.

While the patties are cooking, lightly toast your buns.

To build your burger, start with your toasted bun base, add a tablespoon of special sauce, then top with slices of tomato and red onion, as well as some iceberg. Stack the three burgers on top and finish with the bun lid.

@JACKSMEATSHACK

JEN HARRISON

AIR FRYER QUEEN

Jen Harrison – known to her 160,000 followers on TikTok as @airfry_jen – is a busy mum who has accumulated thousands of followers on social media thanks to her air fryer videos that aim to help make life easier.

36-year-old Jen Harrison lives in Darlington in the north-east of England, where she enjoys a busy family life with husband Ste, juggling her full-time job and looking after her two daughters and step-daughter, Amelia, Alice and Lily, as well as their crazy dog Daisy.

"I started cooking with my air fryer in June 2022 following urgent spinal surgery due to a slipped disc in my spinal cord," says Jen. "During the recovery, my mobility was massively reduced and I could not lift or hold anything too heavy. Around the same time, my husband won an award at work and received some gift vouchers – he bought a Ninja dual air fryer, as it could sit on the worktop and would be easier for me to use than lifting things in and out of the oven."

Jen admits she wasn't particularly bothered about trying the air fryer at first. However, after mentioning it to some friends on the school run, one of her mum friends said you could cook a full chicken in one. "I didn't believe her," laughs Jen, "but I said I would try it and send her a video!"

Before this point, Jen had never posted on TikTok, or used it at all really. She posted the chicken video on there and within hours it had gained thousands of views – and comments from people all over the world. "It went absolutely crazy," says Jen, "so I just started filming each time I cooked, and started accumulating a lot of followers."

As her followers multiplied, it motivated her to keep posting – and within a year she had 160,000 followers! She now uses the air fryer for literally every meal, getting her girls involved and baking things in it too.

"I like to make meals that are realistic for busy working people to cook," explains Jen. "In-between school runs, afterschool clubs and working full time, I don't have much time to prep and cook, like a lot of people, so I enjoy filming and sharing videos of real dinners that may give other people ideas. When I first got my air fryer, I had no clue how to use it, so now it's nice that I can motivate and inspire other people to cook quick and easy dinners with theirs."

JEN HARRISON

BREAKFAST MUFFIN

Prep time: 5 minutes | Cook time: 15-20 minutes | Serves 1

This is an air fried version of the famous classic. If you don't have the sausage meat you can use frozen sausage patties – available from most supermarkets – as an alternative.

100g sausage meat
1 frozen hash brown
Handful of mushrooms
1 medium egg
1 toasting muffin, sliced in half
2 slices of cheese

Make a ball out of the sausage meat and then flatten it into a patty shape. Place the sausage patty, hash brown and mushrooms in the air fryer – if you have a stainless steel rack, use this to create a separate layer for the patty and hash brown, otherwise place in one drawer. Air fry these for 15 minutes at 200°c.

Meanwhile crack the egg into a a silicone Yorkshire pudding or cupcake mould. Air fry this at 180°c for 8 to 10 minutes (depending on how runny you like your egg). If you have a dual drawer air fryer you can do this while the patty and hash brown are cooking.

Place the halved muffin into the air fryer for 3 minutes at 200°c.

Construct your breakfast muffin, placing a slice of cheese on the base of the muffin and topping it with the hash brown, then the patty, then the egg, then the other cheese slice and finally the top of the muffin. Serve with the mushrooms on the side.

JEN HARRISON

CHICKEN AND CHORIZO

Prep time: 10 minutes | Cook time: 25 minutes | Serves 2

Chicken and chorizo together is such a delicious combination! You can throw in any veg you fancy with this.

250g chicken, diced
1 red onion, cut into chunks
1 chorizo ring, cut into chunks
Handful of spinach
100g cherry tomatoes, halved
1 ball of mozzarella, cut into 1cm pieces

Air fry the diced chicken for 10 minutes at 200°c.

Add the onion and chorizo chunks to the chicken and cook all together for a further 10 minutes until cooked through.

Once cooked, add the spinach, halved tomatoes and chopped mozzarella, and air fry for a further 4 minutes. Serve and enjoy!

JEN HARRISON

STEAK AND VEG

Prep time: 2 minutes | Cook time: 7-9 minutes | Serves 1

This is a super quick and easy meal to make in the air fryer; you can pop it all in the same drawer and leave it to cook. Air frying for 7 minutes will give you a medium-rare steak; if you like your steak well done, I would recommend 9 minutes.

125g asparagus
Handful of cherry tomatoes
1 sirloin steak
Salt and black pepper
Splash of soy sauce

Place the vegetables in the air fryer. If you have a stainless-steel rack, use it to create another level and place your steak on the rack. If you do not have a rack, place the steak next to the veg in the air fryer. Season the steak and veg with salt, pepper and soy sauce.

Air fry at 200°c for 7 minutes (for medium-rare), turning the steak over halfway through cooking to ensure it is evenly cooked. Serve and enjoy!

JENNY JEFFERIES

FOR THE LOVE OF THE LAND & SEA

Award-winning food writer Jenny Jefferies had never really considered where her food came from until she met her now-husband, an arable farmer, on a blind date. Since that moment, she has come to share his passion for the land, and is now best known for celebrating our connection to Mother Nature, supporting our food producers, and raising awareness around food provenance through her Instagram page @jennyljefferies.

Food means different things to different people. Although it can be celebratory, religious, communal and important, Jenny Jefferies is aware that it can also mean loneliness, hardship, poverty and death. "Currently our food supply chain is completely fragmented," explains Jenny, "and much more is needed to be done to help distribute food fairly, to reduce our food waste and to support our British food producers – especially our farmers and fishermen. Because without them, there is simply no food."

When Jenny met her husband, she was desperate to share his passion for the land – and to reconnect with it, acknowledging just how disconnected we have all become from Mother Nature. Jenny became dedicated to bridging the urban and rural divide by educating all generations and backgrounds about food provenance.

Jenny is now the award-winning author of four books, which celebrate our farmers and fishermen. For The Love Of The Land, For The Love Of The Sea and their sequels have been a true labour of love. "The opportunity to share these stories and recipes of our rich cultural heritage, traditions and social history has been an absolute joy and a privilege," says Jenny.

As well as her books, Jenny champions these themes through her Instagram, Facebook and Twitter following, as well as writing regular food columns, blogs and articles.

"Social media has become a modern power of responsibility and obligation," she explains. "It is an opportunity for great connection and engagement. When treated with the utmost respect, this modern phenomenon can be extremely significant. I would go as far as saying that it can be life-changing."

Jenny believes that social media platforms can offer us a space for sharing our experiences and knowledge. Everyone loves a good story and that, for Jenny, is what social media is all about: "Knowledge is power, and with social media, we all have that power in our hands. By helping to make the public aware of the hard work involved in putting food on our tables, I am bringing people closer to the food they eat. I dearly hope my children will grow up in a world where we nurture food as much as food nurtures us."

Photo: www.esmerobinson.com

JENNY JEFFERIES

LAMB AND SWEET POTATO HOTPOT

Prep time: 15 minutes | Cook time: 2 hours | Serves 4

The natural sweetness of the sweet potato complements the lamb beautifully, making this dish a real crowd-pleaser. It really is very quick to prepare, simple and delicious – you can't go wrong!

1kg lamb neck fillet, cut into 2cm chunks
Salt and black pepper
1 tbsp vegetable oil
75g butter
150g onions, finely chopped
1 clove of garlic, sliced
4 carrots, finely chopped
1 tbsp plain flour
200ml red wine
400ml lamb stock
2 sprigs of thyme
1kg sweet potatoes, thinly sliced
Green vegetables of your choice, to serve

Preheat the oven to 170°c.

Season the meat with salt and freshly ground black pepper. Heat a large flameproof casserole dish on the hob, then add the oil and a small knob of the butter. Add the lamb and fry until browned all over, then remove from the pan and set aside.

Add the onions, garlic and another knob of the butter to the pan and fry for 2 to 3 minutes, or until lightly browned. Add the carrots and cook for a further minute.

Stir in the flour then gradually add the red wine, stirring until smooth. Add the browned lamb back into the pan with the stock, and season with salt and freshly ground black pepper. Bring to the boil, then stir in the fresh thyme.

Arrange the sliced potatoes on top and dot the surface with the remaining butter. Cover with a lid (or cover tightly with foil) and cook in the preheated oven for 1 hour.

Remove the lid and increase the heat to 200°c, then cook, uncovered, for 30 minutes.

Serve with green vegetables.

JENNY JEFFERIES

BANANA LOAF

Prep time: 15 minutes | Cook time: 50 minutes | Serves 12

We're extremely lucky to live in such a vibrant village and I get asked a lot to make a cake for local events. This is such a joyful and simple 'go to' recipe that my children love to make and eat! I make this frequently, with their help, and it always goes down well. This recipe is in memory of Ruth MacIntyre, a member of the Guild Of Food Writers.

100g butter, softened
50g caster sugar
2 eggs
2 ripe bananas, mashed
225g self-raising flour
1 tsp baking powder
2 tbsp milk

Lightly grease a 900g loaf tin and line with non-stick baking paper. Preheat the oven to 180°c.

Measure out all the ingredients into a mixing bowl and beat together until blended.

Spoon the mixture into the prepared loaf tin and bake in the preheated oven for about 50 minutes until well risen and golden brown.

Leave the loaf to cool in the tin for a few minutes, then turn out onto a wire rack.

Serve warm with a cup of tea and enjoy!

JENNY JEFFERIES

CHOCOLATE PUDDLE PUDDING

Prep time: 15 minutes | Cook time: 40 minutes | Serves 6

I grew up absolutely loving this special chocolate family favourite treat, and I'm very much enjoying passing on this heart-warming tradition to my own children on birthdays and other special occasions.

85g self-raising flour
2 tbsp cocoa powder
Pinch of salt
115g unsalted butter, softened, plus extra for greasing
115g caster sugar
2 eggs, lightly beaten
1 tsp vanilla extract
1-2 tbsp milk/water, as needed

For the sauce
115g soft brown sugar
2 tbsp cocoa powder
285ml hot water

Butter a 2 litre pie dish and set aside. Preheat the oven to 180°c.

Sift the flour, cocoa powder and salt all together into a mixing bowl.

In a separate bowl, cream together the butter and sugar. Beat in the eggs, vanilla extract and a little of the flour mixture. Fold in the rest of the flour mixture, along with the milk or water, and mix until combined.

Spoon the mixture into the buttered pie dish and set aside.

To make the sauce, combine the sugar and cocoa in a bowl, and stir in the hot water until smooth. Pour this sauce over the top of the cake mixture.

Cook in the centre of the preheated oven for 40 minutes. Serve warm with ice cream.

KAREN WRIGHT

MEALS ON THE MOVE

Karen Wright, star of The Great British Bake Off, is a caravan and motorhome enthusiast, as well as an all-round foodie. Through her Instagram page @karenwrightbake, she has discovered a community of like-minded people who share her love for campsite cooking... she's off on a journey and they're all coming for the ride.

Karen Wright nearly didn't bother applying for The Great British Bake Off at all. She knew she was a good baker, but she'd never attempted the myriad of recipes required for the show. In a decision that changed the course of her life, Karen decided to give it a go. She spent weeks working on the classic techniques that she would need for the show, and the effort paid off – Karen appeared on the series in 2018, where she won over the audience with her personality and bakes.

Since then, Karen has stepped away from baking slightly to return to her lifelong love of cooking. She fondly remembers a childhood spent cooking from a kids' cook book, always being keen to help in the kitchen. "I wish I'd kept that cook book," Karen reminisces, "you know, the way you wish you'd kept certain toys?"

"As a child we'd always gone on camping or caravan holidays," says Karen, "and it's something I still absolutely love." However, one thing started niggling at Karen: "We always ate well at home, yet for some reason, on holiday, we'd rely on readymade sauces, tins and packets. Why, I asked myself, don't we want to treat ourselves to nice food while we're away?"

During summer 2023 Karen went on a fantastic trip and spent 30 days travelling Europe in a motorhome, and has devised 30 mouth-watering recipes – one for each day, all suitable for cooking on a stovetop within 30 minutes.

These recipes, along with the accompanying travel blog, will form her first book Meals on the Move: A campsite cooking journey, due to be published in autumn 2023. Karen will take her readers on tour with her, depicting the places she travels, the ingredients she buys and the dishes she creates. Each dish will take inspiration from where it is cooked, so expect delights like French onion soup in Fontainebleau, coq au vin in Burgundy, marry me chicken in Tuscany and bratwurst and stoemp in the Alsace region.

Karen has built a huge following within the camping, caravanning and motorhome community online and is known for sharing her campsite-friendly recipes on her Instagram page @karenwrightbake. Here, Karen has shared a sneak preview of three of the recipes from her upcoming book to give us all a tantalising taste of what's to come.

KAREN WRIGHT

PROVENÇAL CHICKEN

Prep time: 5 minutes | Cook time: 35 minutes | Serves 2

This ever-popular chicken casserole from Provence is rich and red in colour. It's another plate of sunshine to enjoy outside in the southern French sunshine.

2 tbsp olive oil
4 boneless and skinless chicken thighs, or breasts
1 onion, sliced
1 red pepper, sliced
4 cloves of garlic, crushed
1 tbsp dried oregano
1 tbsp Worcestershire sauce, or tinned anchovies
1 tbsp plain flour
150ml rosé or white wine
500g passata or chopped tomatoes
200ml chicken stock
½ jar sundried tomatoes
1 tbsp tomato ketchup
Handful of black olives
Salt and black pepper
Handful of basil, torn, to garnish

Heat the oil in a large frying pan over a medium heat and brown the chicken on all sides; this takes about 5 minutes. Transfer to a plate and set aside.

Add the onion to the pan and cook on a low heat for about 5 minutes until softened, then add the red pepper and cook for a couple of minutes. Add the garlic, oregano and Worcestershire sauce, then sprinkle over the flour and mix well. Add the wine, passata and chicken stock, and bring to the boil for a few minutes.

Return the chicken to the pan and reduce to a simmer. Cook until the liquid has reduced, and the sauce is quite thick; this takes about 20 minutes.

Add the sundried tomatoes, ketchup and olives, and season well with salt and pepper. Scatter the basil leaves on top just before serving. This works well served with rice or pasta.

@KARENWRIGHTBAKE

KAREN WRIGHT

MUSHROOM BOURGUIGNON

Prep time: 10 minutes | Cook time: 30 minutes | Serves 2

Beef Bourguignon is my signature dish. I developed my version after living on a campsite in Burgundy for six months and sampling the 'real thing' in the campsite restaurant many times. A beef version takes many hours to simmer and become tender and delicious, so I have created this mushroom version, which also happens to be accidentally vegan! If you can only get large shallots, you will need to modify the recipe, either splitting them or using less (if they are large, they take longer to cook). I have been known to halve or quarter an onion, if I can't get shallots at all. Use the leftovers to make oeufs en meurette for breakfast!

2 tbsp garlic-infused oil
1 onion, finely chopped
1 carrot, finely chopped
4 large cloves of garlic, crushed
4 handfuls of mixed mushrooms, roughly chopped into chunks (at least 15)
2 tbsp tomato purée
1 tbsp dried thyme
1 tbsp Dijon mustard
8 small shallots (ideally the size of a small pickled onion)
2 tbsp plain flour
½ bottle of red wine (Burgundy preferably)
250ml vegetable stock
Salt and black pepper
Large handful of parsley, chopped

Heat the oil in a large, lidded frying pan over a low heat. Add the onion and cook on a gentle heat for about 5 minutes until slightly caramelised to allow the sweetness to develop.

Add the carrot, garlic, mushrooms, tomato purée, thyme, mustard, and the peeled shallots, and cook for a few minutes to allow the mushrooms to release their juices. Sprinkle over the flour, which will thicken the sauce, and give it a stir.

Continue to cook until the mushrooms have wilted a bit, then add the wine and stock. Bring to the boil and then reduce to a simmer with the lid partially on.

Cook until everything is starting to become very saucy, then remove the lid and continue to cook gently until the shallots and carrots are tender and the sauce is thick and glossy. Season to taste with salt and pepper and scatter over the chopped parsley.

This goes well with pasta, rice, mash or, of course, a lovely crusty baguette!

Using leftovers

Oeufs en meurette is a Burgundian way of serving poached eggs. If you have some mushroom bourguignon leftovers, they are perfect reheated for breakfast or lunch the next day. Serve the mushroom bourguignon on a thick slice of white toast, drizzle with extra virgin olive oil, and top with one or two poached eggs and a garnish of parsley.

KAREN WRIGHT

BRATWURST IN BEER WITH STOEMP

Prep time: 10 minutes | Cook time: 30 minutes | Serves 2

Let's start by saying, for bratwurst, say sausages. Any sausages, but ideally fat, porky and herby (or vegetarian, of course). This is a French/Belgian/German dish; it respects no boundaries. The stoemp is what we might describe as bubble and squeak or champ. In northern France, close to the Belgian and German border, stoemp is very common. Cooked root vegetables, leeks and onions, mashed and then fried a bit to crisp up. You can use leftover cooked veg as you would with bubble! I don't peel my potatoes or carrots.

For the stoemp
1 tbsp oil
1 leek, thinly sliced
Salt and black pepper
2 big potatoes, unpeeled and diced
2 carrots, unpeeled and diced
Large knob of butter
Splash of milk
½ tsp grated nutmeg (optional)
Handful of grated cheese (optional)

For the sausages
1 tbsp olive oil
4 fat bratwurst/pork sausages/vegetarian sausages
2 onions, thinly sliced into rings
1 tsp wholegrain mustard
1 stock cube (beef or vegetable)
1 tsp smoked paprika
1 tbsp plain flour
500ml wheat beer
Salt and freshly ground pepper

For the stoemp

Heat the oil in a pan, add the leek and cook for a few minutes until it is tender. Transfer to a plate and set aside.

Fill a large pan with boiling water and add 1 teaspoon of salt. Place the diced potatoes and carrots into the pan and bring to a rolling boil, place a lid on the pan and cook for about 20 minutes until tender.

Drain, crush roughly with a fork or spoon (we are not looking for a smooth mash), then return to the pan. Add the cooked leeks and stir, then add the butter, milk, nutmeg (if using) and cheese (if using), and season well with salt and pepper. Keep warm.

For the sausages

Heat the oil in a frying pan and brown the sausages on all sides. Transfer to a plate and set aside.

Add the sliced onions to the pan and cook on a gentle heat until they are soft and translucent.

Add the mustard, stock cube and the smoked paprika, and stir in. Sprinkle over the flour and mix in. Pour in the beer and bring to a boil, then return the sausages to the pan, reduce the heat to a rolling boil and cook until the beer has reduced by about half and the sausages are cooked through. Season to taste with salt and pepper and serve with the stoemp.

@KARENWRIGHTBAKE

KATHRYN CORNWELL

FOOD FOR HEALTH

Having been diagnosed with IBS as a teenager, and later with coeliac disease, Kathryn Cornwell's health challenges led her to discover the powerful impact food can have on overall wellbeing. This prompted her to take control of her health and inspired her to delve into the realms of gut health and anti-inflammatory eating through her Instagram page @nutritional_life_ltd_.

Kathryn set up Nutritional-life.com when she qualified as a Functional Nutrition Coach. Kathryn's mission is to empower others to prioritise health through food, by sharing a wealth of recipe ideas that not only nourish the body, but taste great too.

It was Kathryn's friends who suggested she start a blog. She admits she wasn't convinced at first, but, during the Covid-19 lockdown in 2020, she decided to give it a go – and it's safe to say she's not looked back. Kathryn started out on Instagram under the name @happycoeliac, but has since become @nutritional_life_ltd_, a name she feels more strongly identifies with what she is about, particularly her commitment to inclusivity. While coeliacs form a significant part of her audience, she ensures her recipes cater for anyone seeking healthy and flavourful dishes.

Kathryn takes notice of what ingredients are hidden in foods. "I took control of my own health through food," she explains, "I am a goal-driven person, so I tasked myself with making myself feel as well as I possibly could, as well as increasing my energy levels. I became acutely aware of all the refined sugars, inflammatory oils and additives that are hidden in food."

For Kathryn, food is medicine that can heal and fuel the body, and from her Instagram page it is evident that her food is beautiful and delicious too. Her page has a global reach, with followers from all over the world, fostering a sense of community.

"I try to make it all as useful as possible," Kathryn says, "with plenty of time and money-saving tips to help integrate healthier choices in everyday lives." One day, she would love to collate all her recipes into her own cook book, putting together a truly inclusive, truly gut-healthy, truly delicious collection of food – and over the next few pages she treats us to a sample of her delectable dishes, from a fresh salad and nourishing soup to an irresistibly healthy flapjack.

KATHRYN CORNWELL

HEALTHIER FLAPJACK

Prep time: 10 minutes, plus 25 minutes setting | Cook time: 20 minutes | Serves 8

Need inspiration for an after-school snack, something for the lunchbox or just a midweek treat? This is a family favourite that has all the flavour of flapjack, but is made using healthier ingredients. The added chia seeds give this flapjack a great level of fibre to aid digestion, and the maca powder has excellent anti-inflammatory properties.

100g odourless coconut oil
70g coconut sugar
80g honey
2 tbsp bovine collagen powder
1 tsp maca powder
1 tsp vanilla extract
220g oats (use gluten-free-certified oats, if needed)
2 tbsp chia seeds

For the topping
35g raw dark chocolate (I use one with no refined sugar)
1 tsp odourless coconut oil

Line a baking tray (18 x 25cm) with parchment paper and preheat the oven to 150°c fan.

Put all the ingredients, except the oats and chia seeds, in a saucepan and place on a low heat to melt. Once melted, remove from the heat and add the oats and chia seeds. Mix well and transfer to the lined baking tray.

Cook in the preheated oven for 20 minutes.

Keep the flapjacks in the tray and cut into eight equal pieces. Chill in the fridge for 20 minutes.

For the topping, melt the chocolate and coconut oil in a bain-marie (a heatproof bowl over a pan of simmering water, making sure the bottom of the bowl doesn't touch the water).

Remove the flapjack from the tray using the parchment paper and carefully break it into the slices. Drizzle with the melted chocolate and leave to set in the fridge for 5 minutes.

KATHRYN CORNWELL

DUCK AND WATERMELON SALAD

Prep time: 20 minutes | Cook time: 3 hours 10 minutes | Serves 4

This is a salad that will liven up your taste buds. It provides a wonderful rollercoaster for the senses with the richness of the duck, the refreshing quality of the watermelon, the freshness of the mint, the crunch of the cashews and the zing from the lime. Chinese five spice and star anise add a sweet and warm flavour, but also have potent anti-inflammatory effects.

4 duck legs
Sea salt
2 tbsp Chinese five spice
2 tbsp soy sauce, or use tamari for gluten-free
1 tbsp honey
1 tbsp mirin
Thumbnail-sized piece of ginger, peeled and grated
1-2 cloves of garlic, peeled and grated
4 star anise
2 big handfuls of raw unsalted cashew nuts
4 big handful of salad leaves
200g watermelon chunks
4 sprigs of mint, leaves only, some shredded
½ lime, juiced
Chilli flakes, to taste (optional)

Preheat the oven to 140°c fan.

Start by generously seasoning the duck legs with sea salt and placing them in a baking dish. Mix together the Chinese five spice, soy sauce, honey, mirin, ginger and garlic in a bowl. Brush this mixture all over the duck legs. Place the star anise amongst the duck. Bake in the preheated oven for 3 hours.

Use a knife and fork to shred the duck. Remove the bones and the star anise.

Increase the oven temperature to 180°c fan. Put the cashew nuts in a dish and bake for 5 to 8 minutes – keep an eye on them as they can easily burn. Give them a shake halfway through the cooking process.

To serve, arrange the salad leaves on the serving plates, top with shredded duck, watermelon and cashew nuts. Scatter the mint leaves (a mix of whole and shredded leaves) on top and add a squeeze of lime juice and a pinch of chilli flakes, if you like.

KATHRYN CORNWELL

CREAMY ROASTED TOMATO SOUP

Prep time: 30 minutes | Cook time: 1 hour 10 minutes | Serves 2-4

There's nothing more delicious than a homemade tomato soup. This creamy dairy-free soup is comfort food at its best. Tomatoes are full of antioxidants to support your cell and brain health, as well as boosting your mood. The bone broth is full of glycine, which reduces inflammation in your gut, as well as gut-healing gelatine.

500g tomatoes, halved

1 red bell pepper, halved and deseeded

1 red onion, quartered

1 bulb of garlic, halved

3-5 sprigs each of rosemary and thyme, plus extra to serve

Sea salt and black pepper

1-2 tbsp olive oil

1 x 400g tin of coconut milk

100ml chicken bone broth

1 tbsp gluten-free Worcestershire sauce

1 tsp ground turmeric

1 tsp paprika

1 tsp coconut sugar

Basil oil, to serve

Preheat the oven to 160°c fan.

Put the tomatoes, pepper, onion, garlic, rosemary and thyme onto a baking tray. Season with sea salt and black pepper and drizzle over the olive oil. Bake in the preheated oven for 1 hour, then allow to cool.

Once cool, remove the skins from the tomatoes and pepper, discard and put the tomatoes and pepper into a saucepan. Squeeze the garlic cloves out of the bulb into the saucepan and discard the bulb. Discard the herb stalks. Deglaze the baking tray with a splash of hot water and use a metal spoon to scrape up all the bits. These bits are flavour bombs! Pour this into the saucepan and add the coconut milk, bone broth, gluten-free Worcestershire sauce, turmeric, paprika and coconut sugar. Warm on a medium heat, but don't let it boil.

Blitz until smooth with a hand blender, then taste and adjust with more sea salt if needed.

Serve piping hot with a drizzle of basil oil and a sprig of thyme.

LINDSEY WILLIS

HEALTHY AND HAPPY

Lindsey Willis started her weight loss journey back in 2013, inspired to become healthier for her daughters. A previously self-proclaimed 'beige' food binger, Lindsey set up her Instagram account @slimming.gym.and.gin as a way of keeping herself accountable in her new healthy eating lifestyle. Recreating the food she loves in a low calorie way and refraining from putting any food on an off-limits list is the cornerstone of her account.

Rewind to 10 years ago and you would find a very different Lindsey Willis to the the person she is now. Her diet previously consisted of oven-cooked food lacking in nutrition and greasy takeaways. Her cooking skills certainly left a lot to be desired! But today, spurred on by the birth of her daughters, Lindsey @slimming.gym.and.gin has developed ways to enjoy all the foods that she loved before, just cooked from scratch, and using healthier ingredients.

Away from her account Lindsey is a busy mum of two little ladies who spends a lot of time experimenting in the kitchen. Between being a full-time chauffeur, running a busy household and working in sales and marketing, Lindsey had always dreamt of following her passion for food. The cook, photographer, and recipe creator behind @slimming.gym.and.gin. carefully curates recipes to encourage others to enjoy experimenting, recreating and taste-testing the dishes she shares.

Over on her Instagram Lindsey shares meal ideas and recipes to help inspire others to recreate healthy and delicious food at home. Advocating that no food has to be off the menu when trying to eat a little healthier, she shares recipes for many of the nation's favourite dishes. "I started recreating my favourite meals at home while adapting them to make them healthier – this has helped me to lose five stone and keep the weight off!"

You will find lots of easy to recreate 'fakeaway' inspired dishes from all over the world @slimming.gym.and.gin along with a few home comforts thrown in for good measure. The recipes are all calorie and macro counted to help anyone who is on their own weight loss journey, or just trying to eat a little better.

LINDSEY WILLIS

CHILLI BUTTER CHICKEN

Prep time: 5 minutes | Cook time: 15 minutes | Serves 3

Not to be confused with Murgh Makhani, this delicious Chilli Butter Chicken recipe (without cream) is an indulgent yet low calorie twist on one of the nation's favourite takeaway dishes.

3 chicken breast fillets, diced
1 tsp chilli powder, mild
1/3 tsp oregano, dried
1/3 tsp parsley, dried
1 tsp garlic granules
Salt and pepper
Low calorie cooking spray

For the sauce
300ml chicken stock
15ml sriracha hot chilli sauce
1 tbsp runny honey
2 tsp lemon juice
1 tsp oregano, dried
20g buttery light spread
1 tsp chopped garlic
½ tsp chilli paste
Pinch of chilli flakes
1 tbsp cornflour

To garnish
1 spring onion, finely sliced
Sesame seeds

Season the diced chicken breast fillets with the chilli powder, oregano, parsley, garlic granules, salt and pepper.

Heat a pan on the hob over a medium heat and spray with low calorie cooking spray. Stir-fry the chicken until the juices run clear, take off the heat and set aside on a plate.

For the sauce

Make up the chicken stock in a small jug and add the chilli sauce, honey, lemon juice and oregano. Stir to combine.

Place a pan over a low heat and add the buttery spread along with the garlic, chilli paste and chilli flakes. Stir for a minute or so, until the butter has melted, then gradually stir in the stock mixture.

To thicken the sauce, add the cornflour to a mug with a tiny drop of water then mix into a slurry. Pour the slurry into the pan and keep stirring until the sauce reaches your desired consistency.

Toss in the cooked chicken chunks and ensure that the chicken is evenly coated in the sauce.

Remove from the heat and serve immediately with a garnish of spring onion and sesame seeds.

Serve with rice and vegetables of your choice.

Enjoy!

LINDSEY WILLIS

SWEET CHILLI PORK

Prep time: 5 minutes | Cook time: 25 minutes | Serves 2

This sweet and spicy take away-inspired pork tenderloin recipe makes good use of that bottle of sweet chilli sauce that's hiding at the back of your cupboard. It wasn't just made for dipping!

2 tbsp paprika
1 tsp chopped garlic
400g pork tenderloin
Salt and pepper

For the sauce
4 tbsp reduced-sugar sweet chilli sauce
2 tbsp light soy sauce
1 tsp sriracha chilli sauce

To garnish
1 spring onion, finely sliced
1 red chilli pepper, diced

Preheat the air fryer to 180°C.

Rub the paprika and garlic into the pork tenderloin joint and season well with salt and pepper. Place in an ovenproof dish and transfer to the air fryer. Cook for 15 minutes.

While the pork is cooking, add the sweet chilli sauce, soy sauce and sriracha to a small bowl. Mix well to combine.

When the 15 minutes are up, open the air fryer and use a brush to coat the pork in the sauce. Pour any remaining sauce over the top of the pork. Cook for a further 5 minutes at the same temperature.

Remove from the air fryer and allow to rest for around 5 minutes before carving. Drizzle any remaining sauce from the ovenproof dish over the carved pork. Serve with a garnish of finely sliced spring onion, diced red chilli pepper and your own choice of sides.

Enjoy!

LINDSEY WILLIS

HASSELBACK PIZZA STUFFED CHICKEN

Prep time: 10 minutes | Cook time: 20 minutes | Serves 4

Why choose between pizza and chicken when you can have both? The great thing about this recipe is that you can mix and match any of your favourite pizza toppings for an easy midweek meal.

4 chicken breast fillets
Salt and pepper
200g light mozzarella
90g salami slices
100g tomato purée
4 tsp dried oregano
4 tbsp chopped fresh basil

Preheat your oven to 180°c.

At a slight angle, cut five slits into each chicken fillet, making sure not to cut all the way through (the breast should remain attached at the bottom). Season each chicken breast with a pinch of salt and pepper.

Next, slice the mozzarella and cut the salami slices in half. To each incision in the chicken breast, add 1 teaspoon of tomato purée, a slice of salami and a mozzarella slice. Once the incisions are stuffed, season each chicken breast with a teaspoon of dried oregano.

Place the chicken breasts in an ovenproof dish, cover with tinfoil and transfer to the hot oven. Cook for 10 minutes at 180°c.

Once the 10 minutes is over, remove the chicken from the oven, discard the tinfoil and return to the oven (uncovered) for a further 8 minutes, or until the juices run clear.

Serve with a garnish of fresh basil and a large helping of side salad.

Enjoy!

LUCY PARR

THE FRIENDLY BAKER

Lucy Parr is known for her delicious home baking and cooking which is all allergy-friendly and vegetarian, inspired by her Cordon Bleu patisserie training and family life. Friendly by name and nature, her Instagram account @lucysfriendlyfoods and very own cookbook, The Friendly Baker, are packed with inspiration for delicious snacks and treats that mean no one has to miss out.

Lucy has loved to cook since receiving her Brownies baking badge aged eight, having experienced the joy of creating something that other people wanted to eat. She spent many happy teenage hours delving into her mother's large collection of 1970s Cordon Bleu magazines, an affiliation that continued when Lucy attended Le Cordon Bleu culinary school in London after graduating from university. Having studied both cuisine and patisserie, she returned to study for a certificate in their innovative plant-based patisserie course, cementing her passion for food.

Lucy is now known as a recipe creator and author of The Friendly Baker, a cookbook published in 2022 that boasts over 75 naturally plant-based recipes for the whole family to enjoy. Lucy's cooking and baking is 'friendly' because her recipes cater for various common allergies and intolerances including dairy, egg, peanut, and sesame. The catalyst for this change of direction in her kitchen was her eldest daughter's diagnosis with severe milk and egg allergies, turning Lucy's cooking on its head.

"I'm a confident, capable, and experimental cook but I was completely out of my depth as to how to cater well for my daughter. It was a massive challenge and I really struggled at first." When her second daughter was diagnosed with peanut and sesame allergies in addition to milk and egg, Lucy realised how few bought foods were left available to them and became acutely aware of how this might mean her girls would miss out, especially when it came to those important social occasions.

Determined not to let this happen, in 2012 Lucy started writing a blog called Lucy's Friendly Foods to document their journey and share her alternative recipes with other families in similar situations. Her debut cookbook contains recipes gathered over ten years from her blog alongside brand new recipes, featuring all the sweet treats you can imagine plus family-friendly meals and savoury snacks. Her popular blog and Instagram page have not only led to collaborations with well-known brands including Waitrose and Nomo, but also made Lucy and her friendly foods an integral part of the allergy-friendly and plant-based community across the internet, bringing everyone along on her cooking and baking journey.

LUCY PARR

SWEETCORN FRITTERS & SPICY TOMATO RELISH

Prep time: 15 minutes | Cook time: 25 minutes | Serves 4

These were one of the first recipes I ever created, and they've been on repeat ever since. Fritters make a great addition to a fried breakfast or brunch, a light and tasty lunch with a salsa and salad, or a superior filling for a vegetarian wrap. The spicy tomato relish makes a lovely, vibrant addition to these fritters but also goes perfectly with vegetarian sausages and burgers.

For the sweetcorn fritters
80g plain flour
1 tbsp baking powder
¼ tsp salt
100ml water
1 small tin of sweetcorn (140g drained weight)
1-2 tbsp flavourless oil, for frying

For the spicy tomato relish
2 shallots, finely chopped
1 clove of garlic, crushed
½ tbsp olive oil
100g cherry tomatoes, roughly chopped
1 tsp red wine vinegar
1 tsp sugar
½ tsp smoked paprika
1 dried chilli, crushed
Salt and pepper

For the sweetcorn fritters

Sift the dry ingredients into a bowl, then stir in the water to make a smooth but thick paste. Stir in the sweetcorn.

Heat 1 tablespoon of oil in a frying pan. Once hot, drop in dollops of the batter and fry until golden on both sides. Add more oil for the second batch if the pan is looking dry. Serve hot.

Variations:

Use any veg you like in these fritters. Grated courgette, defrosted peas or even grated carrot are all good choices. Alternatively, try adding chopped chilli, spring onions and coriander to the sweetcorn version for extra flavour.

For the spicy tomato relish

Sauté the shallot and garlic in the olive oil until fragrant but not coloured.

Add the tomatoes, vinegar, sugar, smoked paprika and dried chilli. Season with a little salt and pepper, stirring everything well.

Simmer gently for 10 minutes until the mixture is jam-like.

Allow the relish to cool, then taste and adjust the seasoning if required.

@LUCYSFRIENDLYFOODS

LEMON SHERBET DRIZZLE CAKE

Prep time: 15 minutes | Baking time: 30 minutes | Makes 1 x 2 lb/1kg loaf cake

What could be better than a light lemon sponge drizzled with a citrus sherbet syrup, creating the ultimate sweet but zippy lemon flavour and a sticky, gooey top? This cake really packs in the zing, and it's been the family favourite for many years, wheeled out for any celebration when a chocolate cake doesn't quite fit. Try it, you'll love it!

200g self-raising flour
½ tsp bicarbonate of soda
¼ tsp salt
100g caster sugar
1 unwaxed lemon, zested
150ml dairy-free milk
100ml sunflower oil
1 tsp lemon juice

For the syrup
2½ unwaxed lemons, zested and juiced (approx. 100ml)
100g icing sugar

Preheat the oven to 180°c. Sift the flour, bicarbonate of soda and salt into a bowl. Stir in the sugar and lemon zest.

In a separate bowl, combine the dairy-free milk, sunflower oil and lemon juice.

Make a well in the centre of the dry ingredients and pour the wet ingredients into it. Stir gently until combined into a smooth mixture.

Pour the batter into a lined loaf tin and bake in the preheated oven for 30 minutes (until a thin knife comes out clean).

While the cake is baking, make the syrup. Combine the lemon zest, juice and icing sugar in a saucepan. Bring to the boil and simmer until gorgeously syrupy.

When the cake is cooked, take it out of the oven but leave in the tin and stab the top all over with a knife. Evenly pour over the syrup and then leave to cool in the tin.

Remove the cake from the tin when cooled and dust the top with icing sugar, if desired.

Variations:
Why not try an orange sherbet cake instead? Simply substitute oranges for lemons, using the zest and juice of just one orange to make the syrup.

LUCY PARR

CRÈME BRÛLÉE WITH SHORTBREAD BITES

Prep time: 50 minutes plus 1 hour chilling | Baking time: 10-12 minutes | Serves 4 and makes 20 biscuits

Crème brûlée is an unfailingly popular dessert, so I had to make my own friendly version. A rich, unctuous, vanilla-scented cream topped with a wonderfully crisp glaze to crack... pudding perfection! Why not serve it with some shortbread bites for a lovely textural contrast?

For the crème brûlée
1½ tbsp cornflour
1½ tbsp dairy-free milk
250ml dairy-free double cream
45g caster sugar
1 tsp vanilla extract, or the seeds scraped from ½ a vanilla pod
2 tbsp granulated sugar

For the shortbread bites
75g soft brown sugar
1 tsp vanilla extract
¼ tsp salt
225g plain flour
150g dairy-free butter
1 tbsp crunchy sugar, such as demerara or granulated (optional)

For the crème brûlée
Mix the cornflour and milk together to form a smooth liquid, then set aside.
Heat the cream with the sugar until the sugar has dissolved, then stir in the vanilla. Next, stir in the cornflour mix and increase the heat. Whisk until the cream has thickened to a thick yoghurt consistency. This should happen once the mixture comes to a boil.
Pour the creamy mixture into 4 ramekins and place in the fridge to firm up. Once set, sprinkle an even layer of granulated sugar over the top.
Caramelise with a blow torch or under the grill. Eat within an hour to make sure the caramel remains crispy. If eating the next day, prepare the set custard and then add the sugar and grill or blowtorch it just before serving.
Variations: Why not add a small handful of raspberries to the ramekins under the custard, or perhaps add lemon zest instead of the vanilla. Another nice variation is using espresso coffee rather than the milk to slake the cornflour, to make a rather delightful coffee crème brûlée.

For the shortbread bites
Heat the oven to 160°C and line a baking sheet with parchment paper.
Stir the sugar, vanilla, and salt into the flour. Rub in the butter with your fingertips (you need a light touch with shortbread) and then squeeze gently to form a crumbly dough. Roll out the dough between two sheets of parchment paper and then sprinkle with the crunchy sugar. Roll out a little more until it is 0.5cm thick and then chill in the fridge for 20 minutes.
Stamp out or cut out small shapes from the chilled dough. Place on the lined baking sheet and bake for 10-12 minutes, then leave to cool on a wire rack.
Variations: Why not use the zest of a lemon instead of the vanilla or add half a teaspoon of ground cinnamon for some mellow spice.

NATALIE MARTEN

FITNESS, FOOD AND FAMILY

Recipe writer, food photographer and content creator Natalie Marten, known online as @windsor__foodie, reignited her childhood love of cooking when she began to document her family-friendly healthy meals on Instagram… and is followed by thousands of people who love her approach to staying fit while enjoying delicious food.

Natalie Marten's interest in food began as a child, watching her mother cook and bake in the kitchen. "I remember wanting to get involved," says Natalie, "mainly because I was given the opportunity to lick the spoon clean of cake batter afterwards!"

"As a teenager, I'd sometimes sneak downstairs at night and make dishes from cookbooks, a favourite being one from the 70s," remembers Natalie. "I forget the name of it now, but it had recipes such as honeycomb, Welsh rarebit and toffee apples. On occasion, I'd make a mistake… and I remember completely ruining one of our saucepans from burning sugar… It was immediately discarded into the bin!"

Natalie began a career in video games after university, and food became a bit of an afterthought. Working long hours with a lengthy commute, it simply wasn't her main focus. In fact, 13 years passed before she started getting back into the kitchen to create her own food again.

Looking back, it was when she met her now husband, Sam, and had her son, Eric, that her passion for cooking was reignited. "I decided to depart my career and focus on motherhood. It was then that I rediscovered my love of home cooking and began my Instagram account @windsor__foodie. It began as a weightloss diary – I'd log my meals as a way to keep myself accountable." The account slowly started attracting like-minded people who were interested in what she was rustling up each day.

During lockdown, Natalie set about teaching herself photography. She bought a secondhand DSLR camera and taught herself how to use it. She fell in love with food photography, finding it a fantastic way to showcase her recipe creations to the world. It was the perfect outlet for a creative foodie.

"To date I've uploaded over 400 recipes, and I'm still trying to improve my photography," says Natalie. "My ambition is to have my own cookbook, taking all the photos myself."

@windsor__foodie is still focused on health and fitness, with the aim of showing people you can eat delicious meals that don't sacrifice flavour and still maintain a healthy lifestyle. Her passion is inspiring thousands of people, and the interaction with followers brings Natalie joy: "When someone messages me and tells me they cooked a recipe of mine and loved it, it's such a wonderful feeling."

NATALIE MARTEN

LEMONY PRAWN SPAGHETTI

Prep time: 5 minutes | Cook time: 15 minutes | Serves 2-3

Fresh and zesty lemon, fat and juicy prawns, and vibrant green vegetables conjure up scenes of al fresco dining in the warm sunshine. This dish pairs beautifully with a chilled glass of white wine. It takes only minutes to cook and is a real crowd-pleaser.

200g dried spaghetti
1½ tbsp extra-virgin olive oil
100g asparagus tips, cut into 7.5cm pieces
225g cooked, peeled jumbo prawns (defrosted if frozen)
1 large clove of garlic, crushed
1 lemon, zested and juiced
A pinch of red chilli flakes
50g petit pois (defrosted if frozen)
2 generous handfuls of rocket leaves
Salt and black pepper

To garnish
Lemon wedges
Extra rocket leaves

Get a large saucepan of water boiling on the hob and add a generous amount of salt. Add the spaghetti and begin cooking according to the packet instructions.

Around 4 minutes before the spaghetti has finished cooking, heat up a large pan over a medium-high heat. Add half a tablespoon of olive oil into the pan and, once it's hot, add the sliced asparagus tips. Fry for 3 minutes, then add the prawns and fry for about 20 seconds. Once any excess liquid comes out from the prawns, carefully drain it off and discard.

Drain the cooked pasta, reserving a little of the pasta water. Add the pasta to the pan with the prawns and give everything a good stir. Season with salt and cracked black pepper, and add the crushed clove of garlic. Fry for 20 seconds until fragrant, then add the peas, lemon juice, lemon zest and a small pinch of chilli flakes. Toss everything together again to distribute the ingredients evenly through the pasta.

Remove from the heat. Drizzle over the remaining 1 tablespoon of olive oil and add the rocket leaves. Give everything one more mix up.

Serve with lemon wedges on the side and a small scattering of extra rocket leaves.

NATALIE MARTEN

SPEEDY BEEF AND PAK CHOI CHOW MEIN

Prep time: 5 minutes | Cook time: 10 minutes | Serves 1-2

These noodles are ridiculously quick to make, but taste amazing. I often rustle these up when I'm short on time, but want a filling and satisfying meal. This will serve one as a main or two as a side dish.

1 nest of medium egg noodles
½ tbsp vegetable oil
150g lean beef steak mince
70g onion, sliced
1 tsp dark soy sauce
A pinch of white pepper
A pinch of MSG (optional)
½ tbsp light soy sauce
1 tbsp shaoxing rice wine
½ tbsp premium oyster sauce
1 tsp sugar
100g pak choi, ends trimmed

To serve
2 spring onions, green part only, thinly sliced
1 tsp chilli crunch oil (see note)

Begin to cook the egg noodles in boiling water according to the packet instructions.

Meanwhile, place a wok over a high heat and add the vegetable oil. Once hot, add the beef mince and the sliced onion. Cook, breaking the mince down into smaller pieces, until almost browned all over, then add the dark soy sauce, white pepper and MSG. Stir and toss in the wok.

Once cooked, drain the noodles and run them under cold water to stop them cooking further. Set aside for later.

Now back to the beef. Add the light soy sauce, shaoxing rice wine, the oyster sauce and sugar. Give everything a good toss in the wok again to coat the beef. Add the pak choi leaves to the wok and stir-fry for 3 minutes until tender.

Add the cooked noodles to the wok. Toss all the ingredients together well and stir-fry for a further minute.

Serve up and garnish with a scattering of spring onion greens. If you like some spice, add a good drizzle of chilli crunch oil over the top. Enjoy!

Note:
Garlic and chilli crunch oil can be purchased online or at many Chinese supermarkets. It adds a real hit of spice and a lovely texture to dishes. If you're not keen on lots of heat, you can omit this ingredient. You can also use a pinch of red chilli flakes with 1 teaspoon sesame oil as an alternative.

NATALIE MARTEN

SERIOUSLY ADDICTIVE TERIYAKI CHICKEN BITES

Prep time: 10 minutes | Cook time: 30 minutes | Serves 3-4

This is one of my most frequently made recipes. Super crunchy and tender morsels of chicken thigh in a sticky, sweet teriyaki sauce. They are dangerously moreish! If you can find some (I purchase mine online, usually from an Asian supermarket), use potato starch instead of cornflour for the coating mixture, as I find it results in extra crispy chicken.

5 boneless, skinless chicken thighs (about 450g), cut into bite-size pieces
1 large egg, beaten

For the coating
4 tbsp potato starch or cornflour
4 tbsp self-raising flour
1 tsp each salt & white pepper

For the teriyaki sauce
4 tbsp light soy sauce
4 tbsp light soft brown sugar
2 tbsp runny honey
1½ tbsp mirin
2 cloves of garlic, crushed
2.5cm piece of ginger, grated
1 tbsp cornflour mixed with 1 tbsp cold water to form a slurry
½ tsp toasted sesame oil
3 tsp sesame seeds

To garnish
2 tsp sesame seeds
4 spring onions, green part only, thinly sliced
A pinch of red chilli flakes (optional)

Make the coating for the chicken by mixing together the potato starch, self-raising flour, salt and pepper. Take the pieces of chicken thigh and first dip into the beaten egg, then into the coating mixture. For this I use tongs to prevent the flour sticking to my hands and making a mess.

Add enough vegetable oil to a wok or heavy-based frying pan to shallow-fry the chicken pieces (about 2cm depth) and heat it up to around 180°C. Use a medium heat on the hob to do this.

As the oil heats up, make the teriyaki sauce by adding the soy, sugar, honey, mirin, garlic and ginger to a bowl. Mix together well, then heat in a small non-stick saucepan. Bring it to a gentle simmer, then add in the cornflour slurry and keep stirring until it is thick, brown and glossy. Keep warm on the hob on a very low heat until ready to use later.

Once the oil in the wok is at the correct temperature, begin to add the coated chicken, working in batches and trying not to overcrowd the pan. Fry for 6 to 7 minutes, turning halfway, until crispy and beautifully golden. Drain the fried chicken on kitchen towel to remove excess oil.

Discard the oil once cooled and wipe any excess oil from the wok/pan. Place it over a low heat and pour in the teriyaki sauce. Add the sesame oil and stir. Bring to a gentle simmer for a minute, stir well, then add the crispy chicken pieces and toss quickly to coat completely in the sauce. Add the 3 teaspoons of sesame seeds and toss to coat the chicken evenly.

Serve up and garnish with the extra 2 teaspoons of sesame seeds, the sliced spring onion greens and a sprinkle of red chilli flakes for a kick of heat, if desired. Serve with steamed long-grain or jasmine rice.

RAHEEL MIRZA

COOKALONG CURRIES

Raheel Mirza, MasterChef contestant, Guinness World Record holder and self-taught cook, has created a wonderfully diverse foodie business since he first appeared on the BBC's iconic cooking competition in 2020.

Sheffield-based Raheel Mirza, founder of The Cookalong Company, has 20 years' experience in the corporate world of learning and development, delivering leadership training and coaching, and has now taken the leap into the world of food. It was his passion for teaching and coaching, blended with his love of cooking, that formed the basis for his new venture. In March 2020, on the day the first nationwide lockdown was announced, Raheel made his appearance on the BBC's MasterChef. Later that year he founded The Cookalong Company.

Raheel grew up surrounded by food, however, his interest in learning how to cook delicious dishes from around the world was ignited when he and his wife Nadia started to experiment with all manner of flavours. Now he loves to share his foodie ideas with his wife and their two children, Isla, 12, and Ivvah, 3 – his harshest critics! His Pakistani heritage has heavily influenced his cooking style, celebrating all aspects of South Asian cuisine, and in particular Punjabi cooking, with its fiery flavours and characteristic use of whole spices. As well as creating recipe packs for traditional dishes – think saag paneer, daal makhani, butter chicken, lamb rogan josh, chicken biryani, tarka daal and aloo gobi – Raheel also hosts live online cookalongs from the comfort of his own kitchen, with the participants joining from their own kitchens. From Sheffield to Rhode Island and Oslo to Lima, this business has truly global reach.

Giving back to the community, promoting wellbeing and supporting charitable causes are all close to Raheel's heart, so he's often found hosting cookalongs in support of an array of charities. In February 2021, he appeared alongside his daughter Isla on the BBC's The One Show to break the Guinness World Record for the most people cooking simultaneously online: they cooked along with over 1000 people from all around the world on a virtual masterclass, and raised vital funds for the NHS Covid-19 charity.

In May 2021, Raheel launched his first cookbook, produced with his daughter Isla - Sugar, Spice & Stockpile: A Taste Pandemic - which features a collection of recipes from lockdown and was the culmination of a year of hard work. The book combines easy-to-follow recipes with stunning photography, bringing the visual appeal of his Instagram account to the pages of a hardback book.

Other aspects of his diverse business see him taking part in food festivals, private dining, cooking at corporate events and hosting many charity fundraisers – from Cancer Research UK to The Brain Charity. Bringing people together, promoting good mental health and fostering positivity through food and cooking is what has inspired so many people to connect with Raheel through social media and beyond.

@RAHEELMIRZACOOKING

RAHEEL MIRZA

PRAWN BIRYANI

Prep time: 20 minutes | Cook time: 40 minutes | Serves 4

A timeless classic that exudes opulence in its look and flavour notes. The powerful flavours of the Kashmiri chilli powder, black cardamom and star anise create a fanfare for your tastebuds and yet the subtlety of the saffron and green cardamom still hold their own in this cacophony of whole and powdered spices.

For the fried onions & rice
3 onions, sliced
400g white basmati rice
2 bay leaves & 2 tsp cumin seeds
3 cloves, 2 tsp salt & 1 star anise
1 black & 2 green cardamom pods
5cm cinnamon stick
A small pinch of saffron

For the prawns
350g raw king prawns
1 tsp each turmeric powder, Kashmiri chilli powder, ground coriander, ground cumin & salt
4 cloves of garlic, crushed
5cm piece ginger, grated
1 green chilli, finely chopped

For the biryani masala sauce
1 black cardamom pod
1 star anise & 2 bay leaves
2 green cardamom pods
2 tsp cumin seeds
3 tomatoes, finely chopped
½ tsp each green cardamom powder, chilli powder & turmeric
1 tsp ground coriander
½ tsp ground cumin
2 tbsp natural yoghurt

Firstly, wash, drain and soak the rice for 20 minutes and soak your saffron in 1-2 tablespoons of warm milk. Then fry the onions in 6-7 tablespoons oil over a medium-high heat until they turn a dark golden-brown colour. Set aside on a plate lined with kitchen towel to drain any excess oil.

Next, make the rice. Fill a large saucepan with cold tap water, 3-5cm from the top of the pan. Bring this to a rolling boil and add all the whole spices and salt except for the saffron milk. Drain the rice from the soaking water and add it to the pan. Let this boil for 7 to 8 minutes with the lid off until the rice is cooked. You can test this by tasting a grain or two or by squeezing a grain or two between your fingers – it should break/mush easily. Drain off the water and leave the rice to cool in the pan with the lid slightly ajar.

Peel and devein your prawns, then marinate by adding all the ingredients for the prawns into a bowl and giving them a thorough mix. Set aside.

To make the biryani masala sauce, heat 1-2 tablespoons of oil in a large frying pan over a medium heat and add all the whole spices. Once these start to change colour and release their aromas, add the tomatoes, and cook for 4-5 minutes until they soften. Next, add the powdered spices and cook for a further 2-3 minutes, then turn the heat down to low and add the yoghurt. Cook this until the moisture evaporates and you start to get a thicker sauce. Add the prawn mixture to the pan and cook for about 6-7 minutes over a medium heat, stirring regularly, until the prawns are cooked through. They should turn opaque and have a nice pink colour to them. Turn the heat off. Now for layering the biryani. Take a large saucepan or casserole dish and start by spooning in a layer of the basmati rice on the bottom of the pan. Spoon over a teaspoon of the saffron milk and then a handful of the fried onions. Top this with a layer of the prawn masala. Now repeat the process until all the rice, saffron milk, fried onions and prawn masala have been used up. The final layer should be a layer of rice, a final sprinkle of saffron milk, some fried onions and a garnish of finely chopped coriander and mint leaves. Serve with a dollop of yoghurt on the side!.

RAHEEL MIRZA

FIVE LENTIL CURRY

Prep time: 10 minutes | Cook time: 35 minutes | Serves 4

This is a creamy and indulgent lentil dish which is superb served with hot chapatis or on plain white basmati rice. The combination of flavours and textures that come from using the different varieties of lentils results in a truly memorable eating experience. This is a mild-medium spiced dish and can be made hotter by sprinkling in 1-2 chopped fresh green chillies just before serving. The lentil mix is a combination of equal quantities of toor daal, moong daal, masoor daal, urad daal and chana daal.

250g mixed lentils
½ tsp turmeric powder
1 tsp salt
2 bay leaves
2 tbsp oil & 4 cloves
1 black cardamom pod
2 green cardamom pods
1 tsp cumin seeds
1 whole dried red chilli
1½ small onions, finely chopped
2 tsp ginger and garlic paste
½ tsp turmeric powder
½ tsp red chilli powder
1 tsp ground coriander
1 tsp ground cumin
1 tsp salt
2 small tomatoes, chopped
½ tsp garam masala powder

For tempering
2 tbsp oil
8-10 small curry leaves
3-4 cloves of garlic, peeled
1 tsp cumin seeds

To serve
Chopped coriander

Place the lentils in a bowl and rinse thoroughly with cold water 4 to 5 times until the water runs almost clear. Transfer them to a large saucepan and add about 1 litre of cold tap water, as well as the turmeric, salt and bay leaves. Bring to a boil then simmer on a medium heat until the lentils are cooked (about 25 to 30 minutes). Add more water if needed. You are looking for a loose and creamy consistency, not too watery or porridge-like. During the process, you will see foamy water rise to the top, which you can skim off, a little at a time. Check they are cooked by tasting them or pinching them between your thumb and forefinger. Turn the heat off and set aside.

In a second saucepan, heat the oil over a low-medium heat, add the cloves, black cardamom, green cardamom, cumin seeds and whole dried red chilli and sauté until they start to change colour slightly and release their aromas. Be careful not to burn them. Add the onion and ginger and garlic paste and cook until the onions are nicely browned – take your time with this step, making sure the onions take on a nice golden brown colour. Add the powdered spices and salt and cook for a further 2 to 3 minutes on a medium heat. Add the tomatoes and cook until softened.

Transfer the cooked lentils into this onion and tomato base and simmer over a low heat for 5 to 10 minutes so that the lentils absorb the flavour of the base. Add the garam masala and stir through, then turn off the heat.

To prepare the tempering oil, add the oil, curry leaves, garlic cloves and cumin seeds into a frying pan and cook over a medium-high heat until the oil is bubbling gently and the ingredients take on a golden brown colour. Very carefully add this oil mixture into the lentil curry. It will splutter and sizzle, which is an indication that you have achieved the desired heat level for the tempering oil to impart flavour into the lentil curry. Finally, sprinkle over the chopped coriander leaves and serve with plain white basmati rice or chapatis. Enjoy!

RAHEEL MIRZA

CHICKEN PALAK

Prep time: 10 minutes | Cook time: 30 minutes | Serves 4

This is a classic dish and one that represents Pakistani cuisine in all its glory – combining protein with vegetables. Palak is just spinach, and is different to saag, which is a purée of a mixture of greens such as spinach, mustard leaves and dill.

For the chicken
1 whole chicken (about 1kg)
1 tbsp ghee (optional)
2 bay leaves
1 tsp cumin seeds
1 tsp fenugreek seeds
2 tsp crushed coriander seeds
2 onions, finely chopped
2.5cm piece ginger, grated
3 cloves of garlic, crushed
1 tsp each turmeric powder, red chilli powder, garam masala & salt
3 tbsp plain natural yoghurt
1 tbsp kasuri methi (dried fenugreek leaves, highly recommended if you can source it – there is no real substitute for this)
Small handful of coriander leaves, finely chopped

For the palak (spinach)
1 tsp oil
2 tsp cumin seeds
1 tsp red chilli flakes, or to taste
3-4 cloves of garlic, thinly sliced
2 bags (about 500g) washed spinach
1 tsp salt
1 tsp ground coriander

Remove the skin from the chicken and joint into 10 to 12 pieces. Set aside. Heat 3 tablespoons of oil and the ghee, if using, in a saucepan over a low heat. Add the bay leaves, cumin seeds, fenugreek seeds and coriander seeds and sauté the whole spices for a minute or two until they start to go slightly darker in colour and start to release their aromas.

Next, add the onions, ginger and garlic and cook until the mixture turns a dark golden-brown colour. This is a very important step and will take about 8 to 10 minutes.

Add the chicken pieces and cook over a medium-high heat until the chicken takes on a brown colour and any moisture is cooked out to leave a drier consistency. Now, turn the heat down to a low-medium heat and add the powdered spices and salt. Cook these for about 3 to 4 minutes, adding a tiny splash of water if required to stop anything from burning.

Reduce the heat further to a low setting and add the yoghurt. Mix this through and cook for a further 4 to 5 minutes until the moisture from the yoghurt has cooked out and the base masala is coating the chicken pieces. Turn the heat off and set aside while you prepare the spinach.

Place a medium saucepan or wok over a low heat and add 2 teaspoons of water along with the oil, cumin seeds, red chilli flakes and sliced garlic. Cook for a minute or so over a medium heat and then gradually add in the spinach leaves, a large handful at a time, until all the spinach leaves have been wilted down in the pan. Season this mixture with the salt and ground coriander and cook for a final 2 to 3 minutes until the spices are combined into the mixture.

Transfer the spinach leaves to a food processor and blend into a thick purée (or leave the leaves as they are for a more textured consistency).

Add the spinach mixture to the chicken and, over a low heat, add in the kasuri methi and chopped coriander leaves. Cook for a final few minutes to incorporate the flavours. Serve with roti, naan or rice and enjoy!

STEPH COX

FUSS-FREE FAMILY FOOD

Lifelong foodie Steph Cox, better known as Instagram's @notsofarmerswife, credits her love of food to spending a lot of time when she was growing up with her nanna, whose fabulous baking and cooking inspired Steph to find real joy in food.

Steph Cox started her Instagram page @notsofarmerswife back in 2017 when she bought her first home with her partner Ben. In fact the page initially had very little to do with food at all! However, as time went on, she turned the page towards what she loves. "I decided to share the things I love in life, and generally, that was food," explains Steph. "Cooking it, eating it, creating recipes, photographing them. That's what brings me joy."

Steph has shared much of her life on her page, through her pregnancy and experience as a first-time mum through to weaning and simple family recipes. She is known for her quick and easy dishes that can feed the whole family. "I am always cooking for my toddler Lennie," says Steph, "so hopefully it can help give other busy mums ideas too. I did lots of weaning recipes when Lennie was a baby and now I do lots of toddler-friendly dishes, although most of what I cook is eaten by the whole family. Whatever I'm making, it has to be fuss-free and inexpensive."

She shares things like her weekly food shop and weekly meal plans with her 76,000 followers, providing ideas for family meals while keeping the costs down – something that has become vital for many families as the cost of living has risen so dramatically.

Steph confesses she never expected social media to become her career. Until 2020 she was working as a carer, which she loved, but during the pandemic her page flourished to such an extent that she took the plunge to running @notsofarmerswife as a full-time role. Although the page has grown steadily during the last six years, there have been a few viral videos – such as her famous kebabs, which she's included in this book – that catapulted her page into the news. In 2022 Steph was nominated for a Yorkshire Blogger Award, and she's received the same nomination in 2023.

With another baby on the way, there will be lots more baby and toddler-friendly dishes coming over the next few years, as well as insights into pregnancy, motherhood, family life and, of course, lots of delicious food.

STEPH COX

ONE-POT ITALIAN SAUSAGE ORZO

Prep time: 10 minutes | Cook time: 30 minutes | Serves 4

The perfect quick and easy recipe with minimal washing up! The sausage meat can also be substituted with pork or turkey mince to mix it up a little.

- 1 tsp olive oil
- 375g sausage meat
- 1 white onion, finely chopped
- 250g chestnut mushrooms, sliced
- 3 cloves of garlic, finely chopped
- 1 heaped tsp Italian herbs
- 200g orzo
- 1 chicken stock pot, dissolved in 350ml boiling water
- 3 frozen spinach cubes
- 150ml single cream
- 50g parmesan cheese, plus extra to serve
- Salt and black pepper

Heat the oil in a pan on a medium heat and add the sausage meat. Cook for 5 minutes, breaking up the sausage meat with the back of a wooden spoon.

Add the onion, mushrooms and garlic. Mix together well, then add the Italian seasoning.

Add the orzo and chicken stock to the pan along with the spinach cubes. Cook on a medium heat, covered with a lid, for about 10 minutes until the orzo is cooked.

Remove the lid, mix together well and add the cream and parmesan cheese. Season with salt and pepper to taste.

Serve with a bit of extra parmesan and enjoy!

STEPH COX

LAMB PILAF

Prep time: 10 minutes | Cook time: 30 minutes | Serves 4

I have always been a fan of curry dishes and this one is something a little bit different to a standard curry. If you're not a fan of lamb, then worry not, this dish is also delicious with other meats; try beef or chicken mince! If you like a little extra spice, add a chilli in there too.

200g basmati rice

80g green beans, trimmed and cut in half

400g lamb mince

1 white onion, finely chopped

3 cloves of garlic, finely chopped

1 tsp ground turmeric

1 heaped tbsp curry paste

200g baby plum tomatoes, cut in half

1 chicken stock pot

1 tbsp mango chutney, plus extra to serve

100ml water

Pinch of chilli flakes, to serve (optional)

Cook the rice following the packet instructions, adding the green beans halfway through the cooking time for them to cook together.

Cook the mince in a separate pan, breaking it up with a wooden spoon until browned. With lamb mince, I tend not to add any oil.

Add the onion, garlic, turmeric and curry paste. Mix together well and cook until the onion is soft.

Add the tomatoes, chicken stock pot, mango chutney and water. Cook for 5 to 10 minutes.

Add the cooked rice and beans to the dish and mix together well.

Serve with another dollop of mango chutney. Add a sprinkle of chilli flakes if you like a little spice!

@NOTSOFARMERSWIFE

STEPH COX

FAKEAWAY KEBAB

Prep time: 5 minutes | Cook time: 35 minutes in an air fryer or 7 hours in a slow cooker | Serves 4

This recipe is the recipe that went a little crazy on social media – and went viral for both the air fryer and slow cooker methods!

500g lamb mince
1 vegetable stock pot, dissolved in 50ml boiling water
1 tsp paprika
1 tsp mixed herbs
1 tsp ground cumin
1 tsp garlic powder
1 tsp oregano

To serve
4 pitas
Salad of your choice
Sauces of your choice
Chips

Mix all of the ingredients together well in a bowl. Lay a sheet of foil out and mould the meat into a log shape, then wrap in the foil.

Cook in an air fryer on the air fry setting on 180°c for 35 minutes or in a slow cooker on low for 7 hours. Allow to cool slightly before carving.

Serve in a pita bread with salad, chips and sauces of your choice!

For me, there's no better sauce than garlic sauce with a kebab. I make my own using 3 cloves of garlic, very finely chopped, mixed with 4 tablespoons of mayonnaise.

STUART SNOWDEN

WEIRD AND WONDERFUL

Known for his wacky creations, Stuart Snowden – better known as @grumpynorthernfoodie on Instagram and TikTok – is an experimental cook who puts the fun into food for his 58,000 followers…

Stuart Snowden has always loved food and cooking, having worked in restaurants and bars in the past. However it was actually his home life and desire to cook and eat together as a family – with wife Claire and step-children Emily, 11, and Ollie, 6 – that sparked his passion for creating fun and flavoursome dishes.

He began cooking something new for tea each night and filming it for his Instagram and TikTok pages @grumpynorthernfoodie, where the story of Grumpy Northern Foodie began! The first recipe that went viral was his famous spaghetti pancakes (see overleaf for the recipe), which was a dish his step-kids absolutely loved – and so did his followers.

"I just popped some pancake batter in a squeezy bottle and drizzled it out into spirals onto a flat pan. It cooks in seconds. The kids went absolutely crazy for it," says Stuart, who shared the video on social media and it amassed over 800,000 likes on TikTok.

He's also become known for his imaginative combinations, such full English breakfast noodles. "It was the most bizarre combination, but it worked!" says Stuart. "It's all about having fun and experimenting. Seeing what the kids fancy for tea and thinking of things that you might not ordinarily put together, and just seeing what works."

As well as his wacky creations, Grumpy Northern Foodie is also a go-to resource for quick and easy family meals, particularly using an air fryer for getting food on the table in a flash. "I make quick family meals, sometimes I make healthy meals, sometimes I make indulgent recipes," says Stuart, "but the most important thing is for the food to be fun and tasty and inventive – never boring."

With over 58,000 followers on TikTok, reels have definitely taken over from photos for Stuart, who films in his kitchen on a top-of-the-range smartphone. People like to see recipes come together on a video, seeing step by step how he transforms seemingly mismatched ingredients into ingenious family food.

STUART SNOWDEN

SPAGHETTI PANCAKES

Prep time: 10 minutes, plus 4 hours chilling | Cook time: 30 minutes | Serves 4

Kids go crazy for spaghetti pancakes! Especially covered in chocolate sauce… This recipe is worth the time taken to make and will be eaten within seconds. This one has become a firm Saturday morning favourite in the Grumpy Northern Foodie house… and it's had 17.5 million views on TikTok!

300g self-raising flour
3 eggs
175ml milk
Cooking oil spray
Chocolate sauce (in a squeezy bottle), to serve

For best results, prep this the night before cooking. In a jug, mix the flour, eggs and milk until you create a thick batter. The thicker the better for this recipe – if the batter is not the consistency of thick double cream, add more flour as needed. Pour the mixture into a squeezy bottle (any will do, as long as you can squeeze the batter out of the nozzle – you can use an old ketchup bottle if nothing else to hand). Place in the fridge for a minimum of 4 hours, or preferably overnight, to chill.

Using a flat-top stove or a large frying pan, spray six dashes of spray oil and heat on a medium heat. Be careful not to have the pan smoking, as this will cause the batter to cook too quickly.

Straight from the fridge, squeeze the batter into long lines in the pan in one swift motion. Cook for 30 seconds, then, using tongs, gather the 'spaghetti' up and place in a bowl. Repeat until all the batter is used.

To serve, drizzle the chocolate sauce on top of the spaghetti in a bowl (or get creative with your toppings).

STUART SNOWDEN

SAUSAGE AND MASH-FILLED YORKSHIRE PUDDING

Prep time: 30 minutes | Cook time: 30 minutes | Serves 4-6

Giant Yorkshire puddings are the way forward – this is one of many filled Yorkie pud recipes I have made, and it's one that can be eaten all year round with a classic British filling. This recipe has had 2.5 million views on TikTok! Get creative with your fillings – I have also made a pizza-filled Yorkshire pud in the past!

For the Yorkshire pudding
4 eggs
200ml semi-skimmed milk
200g plain flour
75ml vegetable oil

For the filling
8 sausages
200g peas
300ml gravy, plus extra to serve
4 large baking potatoes, peeled and roughly chopped
100ml milk
50g butter
100g mature cheddar cheese, grated

For the Yorkshire pudding, add the eggs and milk to a jug and whisk until the eggs are mixed in with the milk. Slowly add the flour and keep whisking until the mixture is slightly thick. Place in the fridge for at least 30 minutes.

Preheat the oven to 200°c. Put the oil in a large baking dish and pop it in the oven to heat up. Once the oil is hot, pour in the cold Yorkshire pudding mixture straight from the fridge. Start in the centre of the baking dish and then move to the edges.

Place in the oven and cook until the sides have risen tall over the edge of the baking dish and have turned a golden brown colour.

Meanwhile, cook the sausages in the air fryer or grill until golden brown. Once cooked, chop the sausages into small pieces, approximately six pieces per sausage, and place to one side.

Cook the peas in boiling water and prep your gravy.

Cook the potatoes in boiling water until soft, then drain. Add the milk and butter to the drained potatoes and mash until thick and creamy.

Once the Yorkshire pudding has cooked, drain off any excess oil from the baking dish and the Yorkshire pud. In the middle of the pudding, arrange the sausages, peas and gravy – leaving the tall edges of the Yorkshire pud uncovered. Using a spoon, spread the mash over the top of the mixture all the way to the edges of the Yorkshire pud. Top with cheese and place back in the oven until the cheese has melted.

Serve with extra gravy and veg.

@grumpynorthernfoodie

STUART SNOWDEN

AIR FRYER HUNTER'S CHICKEN POCKETS

Prep time: 20 minutes | Cook time: 30 minutes | Serves 4

Air fryers have transformed cooking, and this recipe is a classic pub meal made into a snack-size pocket to eat on the go or as part of a meal. This recipe uses low-fat ingredients, so is good for the waistline as well.

2 large chicken breasts
200ml smoky BBQ sauce
100g low-fat cheese spread
6 slices of smoked back bacon, all fat removed
3 tortilla wraps
100g reduced-fat cheddar cheese, grated
1 egg, beaten

Cook the chicken in the oven until cooked through, then, using two forks, shred the chicken and add to a saucepan. Place the pan on a medium heat, throw in 100ml of the BBQ sauce and the low-fat cheese spread and mix together. Once warmed through, remove from the heat and set aside.

Cook the bacon slices and, once cooked, cut them in half.

Using a pizza slicer, cut each wrap into quarters.

Take a wrap quarter, add a splash of BBQ sauce and, using a spoon, spread it all over the wrap quarter. Add a half-slice of bacon, placing it towards the curved edge of the wrap. Add a large spoon of the chicken mixture on top of the bacon slice. Sprinkle some of the grated cheese on top of the BBQ chicken mix.

Fold the pointed edge of the wrap quarter over the bottom of the mixture and then tuck the open sides over, creating a pocket over the added ingredients. The BBQ sauce should hold the pocket together. Repeat with the remaining wrap quarters and filling ingredients.

Brush beaten egg over both sides of the pockets and place all the pockets in an air fryer and cook at 180°c for 4 minutes on each side.

Serve with salad and your favourite salad dressing.

ZAK TRAVESS

JUNIOR BAKER

Zak Travess shot to foodie fame on Junior Bake Off in 2019 when he was just 13 years old. Today, the young baker, known on TikTok as @zakbakes and Instagram as @zakbakes_, shares his extraordinary baking and cake decorating skills with over 260,000 followers.

Self-taught baker Zak Travess is an 18-year-old baking enthusiast whose passion for baking and creativity in the kitchen led him to apply for Junior Bake Off. At just 13 years old, his culinary skills and creative flair set him apart from the thousands of applicants and led to him taking his place in the famous tent.

"Being there with Prue Leith, Liam Charles and Harry Hill was an amazing experience, and although I didn't make it to the finals unfortunately, I didn't let that stop me," says Zak. "It was such a huge turning point for me, both for my baking and for my social media."

Astonishingly, nobody in Zak's family is a baker – he is entirely self-taught. He often reflects on how baking has always been important for his mental wellbeing. Taking himself off to the kitchen has always been his place where he can switch off and take a break from the stress of studying – most recently for his A-levels.

The show highlighted Zak's focus and creativity, and portrayed him as someone who is not afraid of a challenge, not afraid of hard work and certainly not afraid of experimenting. "I left the show in bread week, and bread is definitely not my strong point," says Zak. It wasn't the end for Zak's baking career though – far from it!

From that moment, Zak's social media presence really took off – he now has over 60,000 followers on Instagram and over 200,000 followers on TikTok! Both pages became dedicated to his creativity in the kitchen, from his adventures as a Kenwood Junior Ambassador to his exquisitely decorated cakes with his famous chocolate drips. He has made many a special occasion cake and the chocolate drip has become his trademark, temptingly and beautifully drizzled over the side of a cake.

Alongside making a plethora of 18th birthday cakes for friends, Zak likes to take part in charity events. "It's important to give back," says Zak, who is particularly fond of supporting Welwyn Hatfield's Willow Foundation.

At just 18, Zak is certainly one to watch. With over 260,000 followers already across social media, Zak is inspiring future bakers to follow their dreams. Having completed his A-levels, Zak is off to university to study TV production, where he hopes to combine his love of baking with his passion for working in TV, which sounds like a truly winning combination.

@ZAKBAKES_ (INSTAGRAM) | @ZAKBAKES (TIKTOK)

Wendy Gill Photography

ZAK TRAVESS

ROCKY ROAD

Prep time: 30 minutes, plus 3 hours chilling | Serves 9

I like to decorate my rocky road with a drizzle of melted white chocolate and my favourite chocolates on top. Enjoy!

250g dark chocolate
130g unsalted butter
40g golden syrup
200g digestive biscuits
180g mini marshmallows
50g raisins (optional)
30g popcorn (optional)

Grease and line a 20cm square tin.

Put the chocolate, butter and golden syrup in a heatproof bowl and either melt in the microwave in 20 second bursts or over a saucepan of simmering water. Set aside to cool slightly.

In a separate bowl, roughly crush up the biscuits. You don't want to over-crush them, as you want some larger and some smaller pieces to help add a variety of textures. Add the marshmallows, as well as the raisins and popcorn (if using), to the bowl with the crushed biscuits. Mix together. (If you don't like raisins or popcorn, you don't have to add them, but feel free to add anything else you would like, fsuch as nuts!)

Add most of the (slightly cooled) chocolate mixture and keeping some to the side, stir together well until the ingredients are fully coated in the chocolate mix.

Transfer the mixture into the lined tin and compress it down using a spatula or wooden spoon. Add the rest of the chocolate mixture on top – this will help get a nicer top to your rocky road.

Put the rocky road in the fridge for about 3 hours until set, then cut into pieces.

ZAK TRAVESS

CHOCOLATE CUPCAKES

Prep time: 20 minutes | Cook time: 20 minutes | Makes 12

These classic chocolate cupcakes have an optional ganache to drizzle over the top of the buttercream for an extra-special finish – perfect for chocaholics!

120g self-raising flour
20g cocoa powder
140g caster sugar
1 tsp baking powder
40g unsalted butter, softened
1 medium egg
125ml milk
1 tsp vanilla extract
2 tbsp coffee (I make up a small amount of instant coffee)
50g chocolate chips

For the buttercream
150g unsalted butter, softened
300g icing sugar
20g cocoa powder
2 tbsp milk, plus extra if needed

For the chocolate ganache (optional)
50g double cream
50g dark chocolate

To decorate
Sprinkles (optional)

Preheat the oven to 180°C (160°C fan) and line a 12-hole cupcake tray with cupcake cases.

In a bowl combine the flour, cocoa powder, sugar, baking powder and butter, and mix together until the butter is combined with the dry ingredients.

Crack the egg into a jug and add the milk, vanilla and coffee. The coffee will really help enhance that chocolate flavour! Gradually add the wet mix into the dry mix until everything is well combined and smooth. Be careful not to overmix the cake mixture. Fold through the chocolate chips.

Divide the cake mixture amongst the 12 cupcake cases, and bake them for about 20 minutes until a cocktail stick comes out clean. Allow to cool completely.

While the cupcakes are baking, let's make the buttercream! Beat the butter in a stand mixer until super light and fluffy. Then gradually add in the icing sugar. Once all of the sugar has been added, add the cocoa powder and milk to help thin it out. If your buttercream is too stiff, then just add in some more milk.

Put the buttercream into a piping bag and, using your favourite nozzle, pipe designs of your choice onto the cupcakes. Make sure your cupcakes are fully cool before putting the buttercream on, as a warm cake will melt it.

The ganache is completely optional. Put the cream and chocolate into a bowl and microwave for 30 seconds, then mix until the chocolate has fully melted. You should have a smooth and delicious chocolate ganache, which I love to pipe over the buttercream, as I love the effect of the chocolate drizzle. Feel free to add some sprinkles to jazz up your cupcakes! Enjoy!

@ZAKBAKES_ (INSTAGRAM) | @ZAKBAKES (TIKTOK)

ZAK TRAVESS

NO-BAKE VANILLA CHEESECAKE

Prep time: 30 minutes, plus 4 hours chilling | Serves 10-14

This cheesecake is easy to make and looks really pretty decorated with fresh fruit. I like to use blueberries and strawberries, but feel free to use whatever you like!

250g digestive biscuits
100g butter, melted
600g cream cheese
100g icing sugar
2 tsp vanilla extract
280ml double cream
Fruit of your choice, to decorate

Crush up the digestives to fine crumbs, making sure there are no lumps of biscuit remaining. You can use a food processor or bash with a rolling pin.

Add the melted butter to the crushed biscuits and mix to combine. Put this mixture into a 20cm cake tin and compress well using the back of a metal spoon.

In a bowl mix together the cream cheese and icing sugar, then add in the vanilla and double cream and mix until stiff peaks form.

Put the cream cheese mixture into the cake tin and flatten the top. Place in the fridge to set for at least 4 hours, or overnight.

When ready to serve, decorate with fresh fruit – and enjoy!